Yalda Afshoon

A Sorrow Is Hidden in Me

The true story of those who struggled
to gain something that was forbidden!

AUSTIN MACAULEY PUBLISHERS™

LONDON ∗ CAMBRIDGE ∗ NEW YORK ∗ SHARJAH

Table of Contents

Preface   5

Chapter One: Stars Light Up   8

Chapter Two: Perfect on Paper   16

Chapter Three: Touch of Your Hand   20

Chapter Four: Don't Know Why   24

Chapter Five: Denying Every Tear   27

Chapter Six: Busier Than Ever   32

Chapter Seven: Light Up the Dark   35

Chapter Eight: Play Pretend   42

Chapter Nine: Start Another Fire   48

Chapter Ten: For Better or Worse   52

Chapter Eleven: Having Nothing Left   57

Chapter Twelve: Still Breathing   62

Chapter Thirteen: In the Dark   69

Chapter Fourteen: My Love Is Pure   76

Chapter Fifteen: Right to My Heart   81

Chapter Sixteen: Find Your Way Back   90

Chapter Seventeen: The Last Time   97

Chapter Eighteen: Please Talk Back   102

Chapter Nineteen: Truth in Your Eyes   109

Chapter Twenty: If Only I knew   115

Preface

I'm not sure why, but this seems to be my preferred method of communication with my readers. I wish there was a way to get to know each of you individually and establish connections with each of you.

This is the story which I was hesitant to write because I wasn't sure it would turn out the way I had hoped. Yet, as time went on, I realized that everyone must deal with the facts of life, which cannot be avoided by any of us.

Since it was impossible for me to study in a dorm with seven other females as my roommates, I used to go to the library and spend the entire day there. That year, I had to work hard to pass my final exams.

The librarian always let me remain longer and gave me as many books as I needed, and we had a good relationship. One day she told me a tale about some individuals with whom she had once worked.

The fact that their narrative was so unusual and bizarre fascinated me in writing about it, but she insisted that she first have to get permission from the family.

We were all excited and exhausted as we packed and prepared to return to our cities since it was nearly summer and I had finished my finals. We had been informed that the results will be sent to us in a month.

I had a visit from the librarian, who offered me the excellent news that I could write about their tale and would be given any additional materials if I required. The third piece of good news was that I will be able to see a few private journals that would be shared with me very soon.

I was overjoyed to be given another chance to write. The stories seemed to come to me out of nowhere, and I was astonished by how the world functions.

Every life, as I've previously stated, has a unique tale to tell, and it is my responsibility to share it with the world.

Following the publication of *She Has It All, The Tides of the Past, Silver Skies and Stars*, I am sharing another novel with you once more.

We'll cross paths again.
With Love
Yalda

To my mother and sisters, as well as to all the other stunning women who have prioritized the lives of their loved ones, I say thank you.

Chapter One
Stars Light Up

He raised his head to see who it was when the door was knocked!

"Welcome inside," he said.

When the door opened, a young woman with a blue dress, dark hair, and a black eye appeared in front of him.

He tried to recall where he had seen her, but he was unable to do so, and after looking at his laptop once more, he turned to the woman and asked her who she was and what she wanted from him.

"I'm Ocean Roy, I visited a few days ago, and you and your colleagues invited me to begin the digital marketing for your company." The woman was visibly astonished, but she managed to contain her shock and responded.

Collin abruptly stood up, expressed regret for his actions, and motioned for her to sit.

He then began discussing the responsibilities she holds at that company, but Ocean was only attempting to pay attention to his face, his manner of speaking, the movement of his hand, and the scent of his perfume that had taken over the room.

After some time, when Collin questioned if she understood all of her responsibilities, she abruptly realized what she had been missing and apologized for not paying attention to his chats.

Collin was depressed from the start and warned her that if she wanted to work there, she had better open her ears and eyes because if she didn't, no one would be around to keep reminding her of her responsibilities.

Ocean was concerned that she had given her boss the wrong impression from the start. But she had to acknowledge that he was so attractive that nobody, not even she, could live next to him.

She got to her feet and tried to thank him once more for giving her the opportunity to work for him.

She quickly left his room and asked the secretary, "Where shall I go?" because she hadn't listened to what he was saying and didn't know where her office was.

"It is preferable if you go to Mr. Darsh's office as he is the second boss in this company and much simpler to work with," the secretary said while grinning at her. She then made a left-pointing motion.

Ocean was considering whether it would have been better for her if she had instead worked for her uncle's business and reported to her dad, but she felt she had made the right choice.

Darsh appeared to be far larger in size than Collin when she knocked on the door and was invited inside. He also had curly hair, tan skin, and a friendly expression.

He invited her to take a seat and said, "I'd like to know how I may help you?"

"I was with Mr. Collin, but regrettably I got sidetracked and missed out on half of what he was explaining."

Darsh burst up laughing and remarked, "And you have definitely offended him.

"Don't worry at all, everything you need to know is mentioned on these papers, and your office is right next to mine, so if you ever have any questions, please feel free to come by and ask."

Darsh immediately departed after that for Collin's office and entered without knocking.

When Collin spotted Darsh entering the room while he was preoccupied with his laptop and the files nearby, he smiled at him and remarked, "What made you leap to my office out of the blue?"

"Nothing important, darling. I just came to see my annoying and grumpy cousin."

Given that he had other meetings to attend, Collin advised him to leave if he had nothing significant to say.

"Did you notice her attractiveness," Darsh questioned as he sat on the leather couch? "Oh my God, she is incredibly gorgeous. Not to mention, she is respectful and nice. She is unlike any girl I have ever seen."

"Who are you talking about?" Collin questioned.

Darsh became irritated and said, "Obviously about Ocean Roy, the lady you just met and forwarded to me."

"If she just seemed to be another female employee of the organization, what can I do about her?"

Darsh, who was becoming increasingly irritated by Collin's responses, retorted, "You don't understand it, she is not just like anyone else; why are you not getting it, she is unique, she looked utterly different."

"Congratulations! I wish you both happiness," Collin remarked as he clapped his hands.

Darsh simply held his hands in the air in a gesture of surrender before saying, "I give up. Only if you open your eyes and your heart will you be able to see the beauty."

"You simply remind me of my father, who believes he is the only person with brains. If you continue to speak incoherently, I'll kick you out of my office."

"You know very well that we come from a family that has limitations on what kind of woman we can choose to marry; our parents believe in arrange marriages, and this has been the case for many years. None of us can violate the rules or else we will be kicked out and our entire wealth will be taken from us," Darsh said while leaving the room.

Additionally, he warned him against arriving after dinnertime tonight as they were all gathering at Collin's place.

Collin simply nodded in agreement, but he was deep in thought and needed to meet Della, his true love.

***

Collin's father, Mr. Criss, was furious since his one and only son was still away at this point, which was after ten. He lit his cigar and questioned, "Collin has gone to meet that awful girl, hasn't he?" looking at Darsh with a mournful expression.

Darsh's response was an attempt to cover up his confusion by saying, "There has been some extra work in the office and I'm sure Collin has stayed late to finish everything."

Mr. Criss was still angry with his son and demanded that whatever he was doing with the horrible woman has to stop because everyone's life has been negatively impacted by her for more than a year.

Darsh's father, Mr. Mason, attempted to pacify his older brother by inviting him to drink some water and reminding him about Collin's mother, Ava, who was seriously ill and had a poor heart condition.

Mr. Criss was frantically pleading with each one of his family to assist Collin in getting away from that woman before it was too late.

"Our son is no longer a teenager and he has made his choice. He should be the one who can come to the conclusion that that woman, who has already gone through three divorces and has abandoned her five-year-old boy, is not a suitable wife for him," said Ava.

Mr. Criss understood that she was correct, but Collin was so blinded by love that he was also harming his loved ones in addition to himself.

Then he acknowledged, "We were also young people and had all of our ups and downs, but we never went so far as to hurt our family. My wife is ill, and Collin needs to know his mother is priority of his life and do what is right."

Without letting anyone know, Darsh hurriedly grabbed his phone and rushed to the garden to call Collin. "I've already warned you to get home as quickly as possible to avoid another fight."

"I'll be there shortly, but if you don't want me to, I may turn around and return to my home, where my love is staying," Collin responded.

"Your father is waiting to kick you, so please be quiet and arrive early. However, don't start a conversation because you are well aware that your mother recently underwent a heart transplant." He swiftly closed the line and entered before anyone could notice he was missing.

Collin pulled his car over to the side of the road and sat with his head fixed on the steering wheel. He was sick of the arguments and battles, angry with himself, and puzzled as to why Della had to start such a large family feud from the outset. Why couldn't she just consent to his father's requirement, obtain a license to marry, and complete everything?

He could still recall Della telling him, repeatedly, "Don't expect me to say yes to that arrogant old guy demands, I do love you but I am not willing to close my eyes on my dreams and just become a wife and remain at home, I am free woman and no one can tell me what to do, not even you."

"My love, you very well know that none of these arguments are related to my father; rather, I am attempting to go cautiously due to my mother's health issues, if you had just been respectful and maintained a healthy relationship with my mother, at the very least she would have been the one to request that my father come down and bless our wedding, I can't believe how self-centered you were, yet the way you dressed and the insulting comments you made about our religion created all these arguments."

Before he left the house, Della tied him up and grabbed him by the back. She remarked, "You know we both have extremely high expectations in life, if you leave your father because of me, we'll both be disappointed.

"He won't give you anything from the fortune he has amassed up to this point! Why then do you insist on getting married? Let's continue to be lovers while ending our lives as friends in the same home. In this way, we may both benefit from one other's businesses and achieve our goals!"

Collin could not say no to her beauty; he knew she was wrong but he was not prepared to let go of her because she was his first love. He wished Della could have understood his responsibilities in life.

Della requested that he stay at night even though she was fully aware that he had to return to his family because his mother was dying and he didn't want to miss any opportunity to be by her side.

In her last kiss, Della remarked, "I wish you loved me as much as your mother does. I'm extremely lonely and need you too. However, your mother has so many people around her. Just stay longer."

He returned her kiss and promised her for all time that he would be hers forever. All he needed was some time to call the solution, and then they would be together forever.

Collin was feeling extremely exhausted but he had no option but to start the car and head home since he knew that he would have to confront his father and battle over Della once more tonight.

Darsh immediately approached him after spotting his car and asked, "Why have you parked your car in front of the gate when it is your house and you may bring it in, you know that?"

Collin was not in the mood for his jokes, but Darsh persisted, "Since your family has missed you so much, your father has prepared a speech; he can't wait for your arrival, so please hurry up."

Collin gave him the smile he was hoping for when he lost control of himself.

When Collin opened the door and went inside, his sister Olivia was the first person he noticed. She appeared frightened, which Collin deduced meant she was afraid of the impending huge battle.

Collin greeted everyone and apologized for being late before going straight to his mother and giving her a bear embrace.

However, despite being expected to do so after spending time with Della, he showed zero respect for his father and didn't even bother to say hello.

"Where have you been all this time?" his father inquired when he realized he couldn't keep going any longer.

"Why do you want to know where I've gone when you already know?" Ava pleaded with her husband to wait until after dinner and to avoid starting a fight, but it appeared no one could hear her, so he responded.

"You can be mature enough to respond appropriately to the question I asked of you," Criss asked once more.

When Collin noticed that everyone was looking at him, he responded, "I was with my wife and my love in my own home, where I belong. Now are you happy?"

"Shame on you for spending time with such rubbish; if she were a genuine woman, the three men who came before you wouldn't have left her.

"She wants you to pay for her parties and all of her costs; she is here to add money to her bank account before she leaves you behind for someone else. Why can't you see?"

Collin became so enraged that he yelled at his father and started to walk away, but his mother called and asked him to calm down. When he looked at her face, all he could feel was love.

Then he approached her, sat down next to her, and grabbed her hand while saying, "Mom, I'm a grown man. I should be free to choose the lady I love. Why aren't you folks letting me be and simply being supportive?"

While sobbing, his mother hugged him closer to her and said, "My son, I didn't raise you to insult your father. I have correctly taught you our culture and religion. By knowing all that and still neglecting it, it is truly disappointing."

"But mum, I adore her. Why doesn't anyone care about how I feel or what I think? I know she had a nasty history, but now that she's with me, I don't mind what she did previously."

Once more outraged, Mr. Criss continued, "She has abandoned her own son. Have you ever questioned her why all three men before you left her? Why haven't any of her marriages been successful?

"Do you know how your mother wound up in the operating room?" Collin didn't respond to his dad and attempted to avoid him once again when he said this.

"Because of Della, after she visited our home and got into a fight with your mother and I, the two of you departed, and I was left to pick up Ava and take her straight to the emergency, where she eventually ended up."

Collin was thinking a bit and he was remembering the night which Della refused to open a good relationship with his parents, he never knew why without knowing them she was trying to create fight among them.

He therefore reasoned that he should just skip dinner and return to his bed. Darsh followed him as well. Collin had a house next to his father's building that he had just completed furnishing and renovating in the hopes that one day he and Della would be able to live there together.

Darsh came and joined him in the balcony after purifying two glasses of wine. He was completely aware of his situation, yet he was unable to assist Collin.

He was also in love with Olivia, Collin's sister, but according to family rules and because of their intimidation, he was not permitted to even talk about his feelings.

He was terrified since, although getting married with cousins was acceptable in many cultures, he was not one of them. He had to consent when his father was assigned a wife. While Olivia shared his feelings for him, none of them had the strength to express it following Collin's mess-making.

He simply held up his glass and said, "I wish I had the confidence to speak out about the girl I love, but it appears if we talk or if we don't, all the same," before downing the rest of his drink.

Both of them sat on the terrace that night until late.

***

"Please come to my office, Ms. Roy."

The moment Ocean got up to leave, one of the staff members stopped her and comforted her, saying, "Don't worry, you'll get used to his personality, and it'll be simple for you to tolerate his snobbish manner and harsh comments."

Ocean didn't object to his boss's behavior because she believed it to be perfectly appropriate.

She was a little concerned because the last time she was in his office, she became preoccupied by Collin's gaze and entirely missed everything that happened on the first day.

When she knocked on his door, he motioned for her to enter, saying, "Please have a seat."

"I have seen some of the work you have recently completed for us, and I really like the short films and display advertising, they are extremely innovative, I am going to release them today and you can try to post them. My aspirations are very strong, and I want to tell you keep up the fantastic work."

Ocean made a pledge to herself that she would conduct herself professionally in order to appease his boss.

"I simply wanted to describe the promotional massaging and assess its influence on our customers' journeys. I have a lot of work ahead of me, but I've pledged that I won't fail you or your business."

"Wow, that is very significant, and I am delighted. Darsh was done a good choice to recruit you, typically he doesn't do anything right except for this time," said Collin as he pulled out his specs to try to get a closer look at her.

Then both chuckled, and for the first time in almost two months, Ocean had witnessed him smirking.

Although she got up to leave, she held out hope Collin would invite her to stay longer.

After she departed, Collin was still considering her and recalling what Darsh had said about her on the first day, including how unusual and attractive she is. He was willing to agree that there was something exceptional about her.

Della called suddenly and demanded that Collin obtain the key from his father because she wanted to spend weekend at the beach house with her buddy.

He found it hard to believe that she wanted to spend the weekend there and even that she didn't want him to be a part of her plans.

"I'm sorry, dear, but I can't utilize that location since it belongs to my family, not just to me."

"Oh Collin, stop talking like a baby once in a while, and remember that I am a member of your family. I also assumed that you loved me dearly and would never reject me."

Collin merely shook his head and promised to see what he could do.

Chapter Two
Perfect on Paper

Collin was in a bad temper as usual and didn't want to eat when it came time for lunch and all the staff members were in the underground canteen serving it.

He stood up when he heard laughter and made a plan to go see who it was. At least in this way, he could coerce himself to leave his dull room.

He was correct. It was Ocean's voice, and the woman next to her was trying to learn French from her. He was unaware that she was a fluent French speaker.

He was perplexed as to why she never brought up any subject. He questioned the fact that he had a horrible attitude toward her might be the cause.

Collin believed that what the two women were doing during their break time was inappropriate for the workplace and that he needed to give them both a lesson.

He dialed Ocean's landline after returning to his office.

When Ocean saw his name show on the screen of her landline, she became anxious and took up the phone to immediately reassure her buddy. "Ms. Ocean, please come to my office right away."

What could be so urgent that he has asked her to meet him during her break time? She wondered as she kept the phone.

"I believe he's going to fire us," Sophia exclaimed as she rose up to face Ocean.

Ocean burst up laughing and asked, "Since when are staff members fired for laughing? It is preferable to discover the truth rather than make things up."

The door to his room was already left open when she arrived. She knocked, and Collin gave her permission to enter.

She was requested to take the documents from Collin's desk, who was standing by the window and appeared outraged.

"I have folks traveling from Paris for an essential meeting tomorrow, and the company interpreter is off on maternity leave. I have been handling her tasks ever since. I would want to delegate this responsibility to you since you are excellent at singing and cracking jokes in French."

Although Ocean was glad that they had not been fired, she was perplexed as to why they had been penalized for laughing and speaking French, as these actions had nothing to do with Collin or the duties of employments in his office.

"Additionally, Ms. Sofia must prepare a list of our achievements for the previous two years and keep it on my table by evening or else she will be removed."

"Yes, Mr. Collin, I will inform her as well."

She didn't know what had just transpired when she left his room, but she did know that she needed to get to work right now or else she would have to leave too.

Sofia's face was so pale that she appeared terrified. When Ocean entered the room, she hurried over to her and asked, "Are we both fired?"

Ocean held her hand as she described what had occurred and urged her to get started right away since there was lot to do.

Sofia said she would phone her husband to let him know she would be running behind schedule tonight. She was relieved that she could continue working.

Ocean was once more lost in her own world and unsure of why she was so devoted to Collin despite the fact that he had treated her so badly.

She did not feel well about the whole incident and was afraid to say she had fallen in love with him.

She also walked over to her desk and got to work.

After finishing lunch, Darsh walked over to Ocean's desk and inquired as to why they had not joined them for meal.

Sophia responded instead, "Oh Mr. Darsh, we would rather work hard and be more efficient."

Both women started laughing as Darsh continued to look at them in confusion. He then left the room and went straight to Collin's.

"They skipped lunch and are now working extremely hard, so I have no idea what's going on with those two girls."

"I can see you are dying of curiosity," Collin said as he peered at him while checking his emails.

"Tell me, Collin, what have you done to these unfortunate ladies."

"Nothing wrong, I thought to give them a lot of extra work because I saw how carefree and having fun they were. Did you know that Ms. Roy speaks fluent French?"

"How could you punish them," Darsh said, "It was their break time, and they had not broken any business rules. And yes, I knew Ocean speaks French; it was noted on her resume, along with her ability to speak Spanish, Chinese, Arabic, and Persian."

Darsh got up and went to check the door once again to make sure nobody was listening in on their chat.

Then he came back and said, "You need to quit venting your anger on other people, or we'll soon lose all of our dependable staff members, including Ms. Roy, who is a highly smart woman with extremely excellent qualifications. She acknowledged that working for us would pay less than she was entitled to. As a result, if you abandon her, I'll knock you."

Ocean finished translation in an hour and double-checked it before handing it along to be sure she hadn't missed a word.

She went straight to Collin's secretory and requested if she may hand him these documents.

The secretary insisted that Mr. Collin receive all pertinent materials directly.

Ocean was afraid to see him again since she didn't want him to know how she felt about him, but there didn't appear to be any other option.

Collin was already on the phone when she entered, so she left the documents on his desk before exiting, he then asked her to stay until the end of his call.

"I can't believe you finished that quickly; if it had been me, I would have needed a day to complete it. Many thanks."

"Thank you, it was helpful practice for me. If you ever need my assistance again, kindly let me know."

This time, Collin was the one gazing at her, pondering the nature of his feelings for her. Why is she so attractive?

Just realized he must always be truthful to Della.

Then he attempted to make a call while turning to thank her once again.

Ocean also observed something new about him this time, including the way he was gazing, but she was unable to understand why he was clutching to his emotions, why he couldn't just be kind, or perhaps she had to put up with him having such a bad attitude.

Ocean began assisting Sophia, who was delighted because she had a lot of work to do and had no chance of doing it early.

Around seven o'clock in the evening, Collin considered leaving work and going to visit Della since he missed her.

On his way out, he noticed that the two ladies were still at their desks and that no one else was present. Being so ruthless made him feel ashamed of himself. But in order for people to take him seriously and show some respect, he had to maintain some order in his workplace.

Sophia made a cup of tea for herself and Ocean because she was feeling exhausted. As she handed Ocean the cup, she said:

"Ocean, you are extremely talented, and the only person in this huge organization who speaks nearly six languages. I wonder how you landed here, and how you managed to acquire so many languages at once without getting lost."

"I was born in Madrid, Spain, where my family owned a business. I was homeschooled, and I had a lot of spare time, which my parents thought should be used to learn foreign languages to expand our company in the future.

"I'll tell you the remainder of my narrative later; I just need to finish up a little of your work first. Otherwise, we'll wind up sleeping here, so we need to act quickly," stated Ocean.

"If I remain overnight, I'd like to sleep in Mr. Collin's office where I can breathe his perfume and picture him holding me," Sophia remarked, and they both burst out laughing.

Chapter Three
Touch of Your Hand

The following day, Collin requested Ocean to meet him in his office.

She still felt the effects of yesterday's exhaustion because she had to stay and assist Sophia as well as field numerous inquiries from her parents after she got home.

She was intensely concerned that she might have done something wrong again and face punishment.

She was certain that no matter what, she would do everything in her power to make Collin happy since she knew she loved him.

She entered and, as usual, he was preoccupied with the paperwork surrounding him.

The good thing was that Darsh was present in the room, and she felt much more at ease around him than she did with Collin.

Collin was attempting to avoid her or stop looking at her directly since he didn't want to begin developing feelings for a stranger when his true love was already waiting for him!

Ocean was requested to have a seat as Darsh began to discuss the significance of the next meeting and how they needed her to produce various clips from the respective units and activities of their business.

Ocean was taking notes as Collin began to describe how he wanted things done, but even after he finished speaking, she couldn't help but continue to admire him!

Ocean reasoned that it would be best to leave the room before she did anything reckless again.

"I will do my best to provide you anything you have requested. Please give me some time, and I will surely come back to you," she added as she excused herself to leave the room.

Collin continued to focus on the gate, and when Darsh realized this, he approached Collin and said, "Please consider her as your best option. She is great in every aspect. I don't know how you not see all that."

Collin became irritated with him because, despite the fact that he knew she was ideal, she was not the one.

"I find it difficult to comprehend what Della specifically did to you given that you dislike her. You are well aware that I am with her and that she will be my life partner, so stop talking with me about other women or I'll kick you out of my workplace."

"Come on, Collin, I'm your friend, not just your cousin, and I can see how much you've transformed since you started dating Della. You're not spending much time at home or at family events, you're depressed, and you've grown to hate your father. All of this has started since Della entered your life."

In his final words before getting up to depart, Darsh said, "Your family is miserable. How much longer can they stay this way? Until something dreadful occurs, you won't stop.

"Try to open your eyes and discover the real reason Della wants to keep you even though she doesn't want to wed you. I hoped I had not brought you along to that party so you would never meet that woman."

Collin was quiet when Darsh went; it appeared that he already knew everything that Darsh had just told him, but he wanted to be reminded of it.

Why was his life so complicated, he wondered, but he knew one thing for sure: he was no longer happy. At thirty, he felt old and exhausted, transformed, and he knew he was harming his loved ones but he couldn't prevent it or didn't know how.

Ocean was preparing some work and was about to set it down at her table. She wasn't entirely sure what she had added, but she also didn't want to put Collin down in front of the strangers.

After a short while, Darsh called and requested her to join them in the conference room where the guests were waiting.

Before getting up from her desk, she prayed and urged herself not to worry about anything since she needed to be good and stay focused.

In addition to wishing her luck, Sophia advised her to drink some water before leaving.

It was her first time viewing the conference room, which had a large table in the middle, around thirty seats surrounding it, and one large screen in front of which she understood it was her responsibility to connect to her laptop.

Darsh introduced her to everyone at the gathering, including the company owners Mr. Criss (Collin's father) and Mr. Mason (Darsh's father).

"I can't believe my eyes, are you my little Ocean?" Mr. Criss got to his feet and motioned for Ocean to get closer before saying, "Is this a dream?"

"Hello, Uncle Criss. Yes, it's me. I wasn't expecting to see you here."

In front of Collin, he said, "I haven't spoken to your dad in many years, and now that I see you here, I'm wondering why Aiden (Ocean's dad) didn't let me know you were working here."

Collin was not listening at all and was trying to occupy the visitor by translating and explaining a few objects.

Ocean was overcome with emotion and had completely forgotten why she had entered the conference room.

She was encouraged to take a seat and told by Darsh that she could begin whenever she felt ready.

The discussion continued for an hour, and the attendees left satisfied with Ocean's slides and her translations of the various points made during the meeting.

Immediately after the meeting, Collin departed, but Mr. Criss and Mr. Mason invited Ocean to join them for an early supper, and Darsh was delighted to do so. Mr. Criss later called Collin and invited him to join them too.

In the meeting room, the meal was observed before Mr. Criss began to discuss the earlier times.

"We were neighbors, attended the same university, were married the same year, then Aiden decided to move to Spain to finish his studies. I visited them four years later, just as Ocean was starting kindergarten.

"Until I had to stop traveling and care for Collin's mother for the past five years, I used to live with them whenever I traveled to Madrid. When I lost communication with Aiden and his family at this point, it came as a huge shock to me to see you today in my office."

Ocean was feeling uncomfortable as she couldn't even eat since everyone was staring at her.

Although Collin was present, he was not grinning at all.

Ocean eventually made the decision to leave the room and thanked them for lunch.

Mr. Criss assured her that he will soon see her family.

"The last thing you can do right now is to appreciate the lady who has helped us," Darsh said as he gripped Collin's knee underneath the table when they were both seated.

Collin jumped up and said, "Ms. Roy, I truly appreciate all that you accomplished today for the company."

Ocean was overjoyed and thanked him back before departing for the day.

She was ecstatic at home but didn't know how to tell her parents the good news.

"Do you know who owns business I work at?" As she struggled to put on new clothes, she called her mother.

"I believe you said previously that it belonged to that affluent boy," Raya replied (Ocean's mother).

"Yes, but although though he is the CEO, Uncle Criss, dad's friend who used to live with us when we were in Spain, is actually the real owner."

"Oh my God, are you kidding? You've been working at that company for a while now, and you recently learned about him?"

"I never knew the owner would be Uncle Criss, but I'm glad I found out now," Ocean said as she went to sit next to her mother after changing clothes.

"Once he returns from Spain, your dad will be overjoyed, so we must invite them over. I recall that after Criss decided against visiting our home, your dad felt incredibly lonely. Criss was his one and only reliable friend."

Ocean wasn't sure if having them over would change anything about Collin or the way he treated her at work, but she was confident that she could spend enough time in his surroundings to enjoy it.

She used to have a lot of boyfriends, but none of them ever caused her to feel this way. She had never considered this before, and the emotions were brand-new to her.

Chapter Four
Don't Know Why

At the dinner table, Mr. Criss was rambling and reminiscing about the past. Collin wasn't paying much attention, but Ava and Olivia were incredibly interested to hear his tales about the Roy family and the lovely Ocean.

"I adored Raya, Criss, I literally cannot believe we're all back together. She was so beautiful that everyone in the neighborhood was raving about her. I'm sure Ocean looks exactly like her. She is originally from Spain."

Ava was so excited that she devoured everything on her plate as if she had been hungry for days.

"I'm thrilled you found the appropriate person to trust in your office, and she is extremely good at what she does," Mr. Criss stated as he turned to face Collin. "I am very excited for her to join our family. You must make a proposal before others notice her."

Collin became furious and stood up from the table. His mother implored him to stay, but he left anyhow with a few justifications.

***

Collin left his house earlier than usual, but he had no idea what he was looking for or where he needed to go, He made the decision to visit Della while in route, but he was worried that their chat would turn into a dispute and cause another rift in their relationship, which was the last thing he needed at the time.

When he arrived at the office, nobody else was there; instead, he headed straight to Ocean's workplace instead of going to his quarters.

He took up a notebook from her desk after spotting it there and said, "I wish I could understand why he is so frustrated! "He intentionally withheld it. It was her diary, and while he was eager to read the rest of it, he felt that, in his capacity as the company's manager, doing so was quite impolite.

On the table, he also discovered a bottle of perfume. It didn't have a name on it, but when he sniffed it, it was unlike any other fragrance he had ever encountered.

He returned to his office and was just filled with questions in his head. He knew quite well that Ocean was too wonderful to accept, but he had to stick with Della.

He made an effort to stay in his office that day, refusing to answer any calls and letting anybody else in.

He wasn't sure what he was running from or why he had to do it, but he was certain that he needed to stay away from Ocean.

He attempted to phone Della throughout the day, but she was too preoccupied and made an effort to escape him. He wondered what Della might be doing or what could possibly be more valuable to her than he.

He returned home extremely late after leaving the office, and discovered that Olivia had left a message for him.

He was contemplating the fact that this was the final item on his list that he needed to prevent, so he made the decision to leave the house and go locate Della.

He knew that after his parents returned from Ocean's house, the house would no longer bring him calm. He will be questioned about why he didn't show up and why he had again disobeyed his father's wishes.

He arrived at Della's house, a sizable villa in a prime uptown location. The house was owned by Collin and his family, but Della had been residing there for the past few months.

He attempted to unlock the gate but was unsuccessful because he didn't think Della had changed the locks and hadn't even told him.

He waited there for over an hour, but Della didn't return any of his calls.

He was so frustrated and irritated with himself and his miserable life that he was considering how much longer he should put up with his girlfriend's awful attitude.

Collin was attempting to stay in bed as long as possible because it was the weekend, but he received a call from his mother asking him to join them for breakfast.

"Where are you, my brother? I'm terribly missing you. Despite the fact that we share a home, we must keep a note for one another and send letters when we need something."

Collin, who was still in his pajamas, hugged his mother and said, "I'm sorry, my darling. I had a lot of work to accomplish at the office and also went out with some friends after work, so I arrived home really late."

Mr. Criss drank his coffee and sat down on the sofa, igniting his cigar. "Since it is a long weekend and I have invited my buddy Aiden and his family to join us for supper tomorrow night, I ask that you stay at home and refrain from bringing any lame excuses. I want him to accept you as his future son in-law."

Collin wanted to get up from the table as usual when he noticed his mother beckoning for him to take a seat. He sat down at the table since he felt so bad for Ava having to deal with all of this tension.

"I have a wife and I'm devoted to someone else. Have you ever thought about what would happen if Ocean or her family found out about my current relationship with Della?"

"Cheap girls like Della are plentiful in this town, diamonds like Ocean are extremely uncommon, so why should they care about some trash cans like Della, who is not even counted?"

He threw his plate aside and walked away from the table, but Mr. Criss got up and called him back. Olivia was pleading with Collin to stop and think about their mother's situation, but Collin wasn't paying attention.

"I don't care what you do outside of this house; it's my home, and you're still my kid. I have the right to make whatever decisions are best for you, whether you agree with me or not. I will destroy you and your girlfriend if something bad happened to your mother as a result of your behavior, Nevertheless, my home has a respect, so you are free to leave."

Chapter Five
Denying Every Tear

Collin made a promise to himself in the morning that he would first visit Della and understand what she was up to before taking any more action.

When he arrived at her home, Della had the gate open this time. He was unsure of how to approach her yet, on the flip side, he was desperately missing her.

She was greeting him at the door, but she didn't seem very good—she appeared to have been awake the entire night.

"Can you tell me where on earth you've been? How many times should I call you? How many times had you turned down my call? You changed the locks on my house without telling me or even asking me, how dare you?"

"You used to bring me flowers whenever you came, and without kissing me you would never enter the home. It seems like a lot of things have changed on your end as well."

"How many days are you allowing your hubby to spend without you? I'm positive that you are uninterested."

Della sat down next to him on the couch and lit one cigarette before asking, "Which husband goes to sleep at his father's house at night? We are just friends with benefits and both of us decided on it.

"You are a mama's boy and aren't even permitted to move without your foolish father, so how can you call yourself a man!"

Della was aware that she still needed Collin's financial assistance when he got so enraged and stood to leave, to keep him around, she had to think up some intriguing tales other than parties and drugs.

"I want to tell you something, but you have to promise me beforehand that you won't jump to conclusions, so please sit down with me, Collin."

Collin returned and sat at the table after becoming a little more at ease and realizing how much he longed to spend time with her.

Della went and made him a cup of coffee, placed it in front of him, and sat next to him.

"You were aware of my background and where I was born and raised, and you knew that your family wouldn't welcome me from the outset. I've never seen my parents, I was sold by my guardian to a very wealthy club owner, where I've just worked and been trained. I have no idea how to speak or how to dress appropriately."

Collin was in tears while she spoke; he was aware that she had never met her parents, but he was unaware of her involvement with the club.

"The club owner tried to introduce me to some wealthy patrons by bringing them to our venue. However, the rich elderly man quickly fell for me, and I married and divorced him in less than two months. In addition to paying the club owner his share, I was taking half of my husband's fortune with me.

"The last spouse insisted he wanted a child from me, only in that event he would divorce me and give me my half. This is how I wound up divorcing three various people."

Collin was shocked and perplexed as to why he had only learned about these things so recently.

"After that, I made the decision to operate lonely, so I began hosting large gatherings and inviting wealthy gamblers. At one of these gatherings, I met you and thought you might be the best client I've ever had because I was your first love and could effortlessly get anything from you without having to intimidate myself into getting married."

While Della was so calm and serene, as if she were reading a story book, Collin's mouth was open wide because he was so shocked and couldn't believe what he was hearing.

"After spending time with you and getting to know you, I understood for the first time that I had been drawn to you because you stood out among the crowd. Before I met you, I had never experience real love and had no idea what it meant.

"I wanted to stop everything and simply be yours, but after meeting your parents, especially your father, I realized I would not have any place within your family. Instead of waiting and dreaming, I chose to go back to my old life, but this time I won't look for any men since I have you.

"Now is the perfect time to leave if you really want to, since I won't stop you and I won't look for you either," she proclaimed as she stood up and unlocked the door.

Collin pushed her and yelled at her since he was so furious and had not anticipated this. "You very well knew even from the start of our relationship, if you would have informed me, I would have still be with you and your history didn't even matter to me at all, but now you are breaking the news unexpectedly to me, it is so unfair, I deserved better.

"My work isn't done with you, so you have to stay in this partnership until I desire," he said as he walked away while in tears.

He promptly returned to his car and was unaware of what had just occurred! He wasn't sure if Della was speaking the truth, so he tried to persuade himself that she was attempting to paint a negative picture of her history in order get him to stop loving her and quit.

It took him a very long time to put his life back together since he was well aware that if any of these details were revealed to his family, particularly his father, everything in his life would come to an end, and he would also lose his connection with Della forever.

He felt he should assist Della in whatever way because she was up to no good. She could easily be detained and given a lengthy prison term, but he wasn't sure whether he still wanted to be with her because something had shifted inside of him.

He made the decision to leave his car parked and to begin walking because he was afraid and lost and could not go back home because he didn't want to face anyone. He was perplexed as to why his connection with Della had become so difficult.

When his phone rang, it was Olivia asking, "Collin, where are you? I've been itching to talk to you about something for a while, but I've never been able to find the right moment."

"Oh, my dear sister, I'm so sorry. I've been so preoccupied with my own issues that I forgot all about you. Are you alright?"

"Collin, please meet me in 30 minutes at the coffee shop adjacent to the city library. I'll go through everything."

"I'll be there, for sure, sweetheart."

After hearing enough unpleasant news, he hurried to the location, praying it had nothing to do with Della or him.

Collin arrived there to see Olivia waiting there already. "Is everything okay?" he asked as he walked up to the table where she was seated.

"Don't worry brother, when we are at home, it is always you and dad who consistently quarrel, there is no room for me and mom, so I thought if I ask you out, at least we can talk about me and my concerns," Olivia replied with a smile.

Collin gave her a kiss while holding her hand and said, "I'm very sorry about what's been going on. I know I've hurt that family a lot, but I don't know how I can prevent it."

"Now, please put me out of your mind. Tell me, my sister, what's bothering you."

"Collin, I've been in love with Darsh for a long time, and while at first I believed it was simply a feeling that would go away if I ignored it, I've since learned that he is also thinking the same things about me, which just makes me want him more.

"The fact that we are cousins means that our fathers will never permit us to wed, as family marriage is not permitted in our community! I suggested that we leave, but Darsh was not at all open to the idea, claiming that the devastation Collin had already brought upon this family was enough for him to not want to follow in your footsteps.

"Do you know that his father has identified a girl for him, and that they will shortly be getting married?"

Collin simply exhaled heavily and replied, "I'm grateful you trusted me so completely and are sharing this significant aspect of your life with me. To be completely honest, I was aware of this and Darsh had spoken to me as well."

"Oh, Collin I am so relieved because I was afraid you might slap me or denounce me to my father."

"My babysitter, I will never do that. However, I was unable to solve my own situation, so I'm thinking how I may assist you. We must inform both our mother and Darsh's mother; I believe that they will work well together and assist."

"I considered it before, but I was afraid to add another source of stress for mom since I know she has to fight with dad to convince him to accept the truth, and her heart is so frail I can't allow her get involved."

"I am aware that she is not feeling well, but you and I can talk to her and I will try to calm her down. I will also ask Darsh's mother to join us so that you two can talk and let them know.

"For now, this is the only solution I can come up with. The concept of you two running away is not acceptable at all. You know, if I don't see you for one day, I'll know there was something empty in my life. So, let's go home, and I'll promise I'll take action about it."

He pondered his case and Olivia's case the entire drive home. What could he do to make her happy or aid her in any way? He was too preoccupied with his own troubles and those surrounding them to aid his sister at the same time.

Chapter Six
Busier Than Ever

The workplace was busy, and Collin was relieved that Ocean's family had declined his father's offer

Regarding his relationship with Della, he was aware that he needed to act quickly. As usual, the office was full, and several visitors were on their way.

He had planned certain things the previous evening. The first thought that entered his head was to request that Ocean exit.

Even though he felt bad for letting her go and thought she was too good to be true, he was still too angry with her. She was from a very well-known family, she was gorgeous, and she was intelligent, so it didn't take her long to win everyone's hearts, something that Della was never able to do.

He was furious at her introduction into his life at such a delicate time. Despite knowing that he would have to face his father, he had to get rid of her.

He just didn't know where to begin, and he had never been this anxious. He called Ocean and requested her to hurry to his office.

Ocean wondered if the request to visit Collin's office was because she needed to make new preparations for the visitors who would be arriving there soon.

She was relieved that she had at least done something to merit his attention; in this manner, she could gradually express her feelings for him and at the very least, have an opportunity to get to know him better.

"Miss Roy, please take a seat. It has come to my knowledge that the income I am offering you is quite low and the position that you are handling does not correspond to your qualifications."

Ocean's smile vanished as she struggled to comprehend whether the points he was making were beneficial and whether he intended to promote or blame her.

"Unfortunately, I have no choice but to let you go. I am unable to offer you anything at this time, and I am confident that you can easily complain about us to labor as we are exploiting you as something which is not part of your contract. Prior to it being too late, I must let you go."

Ocean's expression altered as she began to cry, but not because of him; instead, she was feeling awful about herself for falling in love with a callous individual like him.

Since she never required the given pay, she spoke up instead of standing and pleading with him to keep her, "We both know that the story is not what it seems to be, and Mr. Collin, you are just being so self-centered to confess it. I apologize to myself for wasting my time and talent working for this organization. I hereby tender my resignation to you."

Darsh entered the room as she was leaving, and he was shocked to see Ocean crying. "Miss Roy, what has happened? I will fix everything, please give me some time," he said.

Everyone was looking at Ocean, wondering what had just happened, but she didn't even respond to Darsh as she headed to her desk to leave!

Sophia rushed over to Ocean and handed her some water, asking, "Is he crazy or what? He was so loud, everyone heard what he just told you. What in the name of God is wrong with him?"

"I can't work in an environment like this. It's best for me to quit."

"Can you explain to me what you did to that girl?" Darsh shouted as he hurriedly burst into the room? "Do you know if this is discovered by your father, both of us will disappear? She is quite helpful to us and we need her. You are being irrational by venting your wrath on the incorrect person."

"Don't even begin; I am confident in what I have accomplished and I am unafraid of what may come next. She had to leave. I had to tell her that she had no place in my life because she was about to take Della's position."

Darsh hastily left the room, hoping to speak with Ocean and convince her to stay, but it was too late and she had already left.

Collin knew exactly what he had done was wrong and that it was unfair to treat a lady in this manner. He also knew that if she had stayed longer, she would have undoubtedly found a way to his heart.

***

Ocean got home but found no one around and went straight to her room. What was he hiding, she wondered, that he needed to get rid of her? She knew she still loved him, and it made her loathe herself even more.

"Ocean honey why are you home soon?" Raya asked.

"Oh, Mom. You being at home surprised me. I decided to depart early because I didn't feel well."

"Yes, my love, you are pretty warm," Raya said as she drew forward and touched Ocean's forehead, adding, "I have told you many times that this job is a great burden and is too much for you."

"I'm sure you're right, mom; perhaps I should give up. I should take some time to relax. I apologize for not communicating with you."

Her mother asked her to take a nap when she left the room. She was worried that if her family found out the truth, they may begin fighting with Collin's parents and she would have to give up on Collin permanently.

She began to question whether she was unattractive enough and whether she was being rejected as she stood in front of the mirror.

Collin never even cared to look into her eyes! "Didn't he think I looked good?" She was wiping away tears as she searched for solutions to her numerous queries.

Chapter Seven
Light Up the Dark

Collin made the decision to put an end to his and Della's game of hide-and-seek the very next day. He rang the bell and promptly went to Della's house, this time without using his keys.

Della was standing at the door when he arrived upstairs.

"I believed you would never return; I feared I had lost you completely."

While holding her in his arms and giving her a kiss, Collin asked her to take a seat.

"My love, you cannot escape me; I am here to show you how much more I love you than before, and I don't care about your past because I want you and I don't want to spend any more time without you. Let's get married as soon as we can."

Della's face was expressionless, as though she were watching the weather channel. "So, I'm finally being accepted by your grouchy father?"

"I'll quit my job and launch my own company with you by my side because I don't care about him anymore."

This time, Della yelled at him, saying, "Collin, please stop daydreaming. I can't keep being married and getting divorced."

"I need to take a break because I'm currently content with my life and considering going alone. We need your father's money to survive, so why do you wish to spoil my happiness?" Della commented.

"Please give us a chance; I'll help you. I swear I'll do everything I can. I can't handle it any longer; I want to be with you forever. Why can't you feel the same way?"

"We are different individuals in this world, I had some unfortunate experiences, and I don't want to hasten anything," Della stated as she went to bring him a glass of wine.

"I do not desire to spend the entirety of my life with one man in one house. I want to be free. I love you, and I want to be at your side, but that doesn't mean we should forego any of the financial support your loving father can give us. If we are wealthy enough, we can live in peace because love cannot satiate all of our needs."

"Do you care that my father wants me to wed someone else, do you even know that he has plans for that?" Collin questioned her.

"So, what, get married, give him what he desires, and soon you can dump her, and suggest that since it didn't work out between you two, we can still be together and benefit from your father's wealth."

In the meantime, Collin had a tape recorder that he put under the sofa and made sure Della wouldn't notice anything about. Della excused herself to go change into her pajamas and promised to return soon.

Della returned in a finely suited outfit, with her face looking angelic with one of the greatest scents of all. She was also quite attractive, with blue eyes, blond hair, and white skin.

She refused Collin's request to give it one more thought, saying instead, "Collin, you are my love, and I am happy this way. Please let's do what the old man want us to do and falsely claim everything is over. On the other side, you initiate investing the funds from your father's business by purchasing plots of land, buildings, and many others.

"We will be very rich soon and then we can stay together and no one will ever come between us again," Della cradled Collin while whispering in his ears. "We will be having all the money we need for our future and our children."

After Collin had been there for a time, Della informed him, "I have seen a penthouse that is furnished with all the amenities and it also has a pool. They have an offer from me, and I also need a little help from you."

"I'll write you a check as soon as you email me the necessary amount." After saying that, Collin walked away.

After Collin left the house, Mr. Criss rang the doorbell right away. Della recognized his voice and invited him inside.

"Welcome, my dear father-in-law; your son just went back. Since I haven't seen you in a while, kindly explain your motivation for being here?"

Mr Criss asked her to quit talking gibberish since he was furious and didn't even want to look at her. "I'm not here to talk to you; I'm here to demand that you leave Collin once and for all. Please let me know what your fee is, and then go off."

"It is not advisable for a gentleman to be seen in my home, what would people say?" Della stated while chuckling so loudly and lighting her cigar.

Mr. Criss spoke the same thing once more, however this time he added, "I don't have any regard for you, and I'm only here to protect my young son from someone as horrible as you because love has rendered him blind and deaf. I'm also here to give you the money you've been waiting for and to get rid of you."

"Oh, Mr. Criss, you are very generous to assist me in this way. However, have you considered your son? What will happen to him if his bride runs away, do you know? Little boy's about to suffer a heart attack!"

"You don't have to stress about him; I know how to fix him. Just leave as soon as you can, and I'll have one condition: you have to pretend you're married and I need to take pictures and films of your ceremony."

Della was laughing like a crazy, she didn't know how to show her happiness, she couldn't believe all what she needed was just in front of her eyes and she just needed to do such a small thing so her dreams could have come true.

Then, she demanded a sizable figure, and Mr. Criss added more than she requested in order to ensure that she would never consider returning.

He threatened to kill her if he learned that she had said anything to Collin about their arrangement.

"Oh Criss, please don't put too much pressure on yourself. Your son is too spoilt to ever be my husband. I can't bear to think of being with him. I'm not interested in getting married to him. But he's crazy and insistent. I hope my disappearance won't harm him too much."

The plans were made, and he stated that after receiving the pictures and videos from her, he would transfer the funds to her account. He also stated that she needed to leave the residence right away and get a new number.

Della happily agreed to his terms and was delighted with the sum of money she would be receiving. She was astounded by how effortlessly the money appeared in her account—no work on her part was required.

***

Collin was reflecting on what had happened over the previous few days while alone in a corner of his room in the evening.

"Can I come in, Collin?" Olivia interrupted his loneliness.

"I must see your lovely face, of course, my sweetheart."

As soon as she entered, Olivia went to the first sofa beside the fireplace and sat down.

"If everything is okay, what has happened to my baby sister?" Collin asked after getting a better look at her.

"Have you considered anything?"

"I have talked to Darsh, and he shares my concept. In fact, he has already told his mother and is waiting to see what she can do. I am preparing to talk to Mum about you tonight, and I want you to be here with me."

Collin laughed as Olivia leaped up, kissed him, and began to dance.

Following some time, Mr. Criss began phoning Collin and asked him to come to the TV room so they could speak.

Collin speculated that perhaps it had to do with Ocean's case at work. He got up from his seat to go to his dad, ready to start a battle, but Olivia prevented him, telling him, "Please don't spoil my joy. You know if you go into that chamber, the tussle will start no matter what. I will tell Dad you are asleep."

"You know our father never quits, so don't panic. Let me go give him what he's been asking for."

Ava was seated in the room and was attempting to soothe her husband down as Mr. Criss was really irate.

"Have you lost your mind?" Mr. Criss asked as soon as he entered the room. "I went to the workplace today, and after I was there for a bit, I learned that Ocean had been fired! She's my closest friend's daughter."

"When did you start having a best friend? Why haven't we ever seen them before? I am the general manager of that company, and this is not the first time I have fired employees. Second, I asked her to go because she wasn't properly perfumed. I was unaware that I needed to respond to you!"

"I am the owner of that business, so I have to know everything about everyone. You understood very well that she was significant to me, and you did this to punish me. Just so you know, you have begun a nasty game with your father."

Collin glanced at his mother, who had her hand on her chest, in a state of such agitation that he decided to stop disputing and return to his lonesome spot.

The following day, he spent a brief amount of time in the office before leaving quickly to visit Della. He understood that at that particular time, the only thing he wanted was to be with her and he was missing her.

When Collin walked into the house, Della had already dressed up and was about to depart.

"Oh, my sweetheart, I was going to go shopping for our new home, I'm hoping you brought your checkbook."

"Allow me to take a seat, then question me about finances." Della began to apologize, and she hung his coat on a hook.

She then proceeded to pour a glass of wine for Collin as always. Instantly, though, her phone rang, and she walked to the room to answer it.

In a hurry, Collin scooped up his recorder, hoping Della wouldn't notice that he had hidden it there.

"I want to stay here tonight; you can go anywhere you wish. I'll go to sleep in a while because I'm too exhausted to go home."

Della was confident that he and his father may quarrel once more, and so he taken shelter at her home.

"Oh sweetheart, I'm so pleased that you finally chose to spend the night here. Don't bother about my shopping; I can do it anytime."

After giving her a kiss and offering her his checkbook, Collin stated, "You can put down the amount you need for the house, and after I have a shower, I'll return and verify it."

Della had no idea how fortunate she had become for this family to give her their fortune without her having to struggle or plead them.

***

After two days, Collin returned home but didn't bother to call his family to let them know what he had been up to. Mr. Criss knew where Collin was, but he expected his son to let him know.

After giving his mother a hug, Collin made plans to head to his room without paying any attention to his father.

"I can't recall what I did wrong to get this kind of behavior from you; I've not raised a son who treats his father with the same disrespect that you do. I am certain that woman is to blame for everything horrible."

Olivia was also there, staring at Collin, who was totally out of his mind. He was strolling in a cloud and not at all displaying any signs of grief or depression as he had two days earlier.

"I don't think I need to explain anything to you going forward; I'm thirty years old and almost married. I wanted to move out a long time ago and have my own place, but you made me come back and live with you. This does not imply that you have to treat me like a fourteen-year-old schoolboy."

Ava couldn't take it anymore and collapsed after witnessing all of these conflicts. Mr. Criss became extremely irate, and he smacked Collin. Collin then pushed his father in self-defense, nearly knocking his head to the ground.

Olivia screamed and hurried to her mother, and Collin followed suit, embracing his mother.

"Collin, even after my passing, you are still not permitted to wed Della. Why don't you let your father be your dad and support you? He knows something that you don't."

Mr. Criss phoned an ambulance when Ava became unconscious.

Ava was immediately transported to the operating room; Olivia was sobbing nonstop while being held by Collin. Mr. Criss was furious with himself because he should have maintained his composure but failed to do so, and now his adoring wife was in the surgery room.

After more than four hours of waiting, the surgeon—who was like a family friend to Mr. Criss—finally emerged.

"Have you made any plans to murder your wife? She is one of my high-risk heart transplant patients, and you knew it. What have you done to her? She is currently preserved, but I don't think she can continue to function as she did before; her activities have been cut in half, and she must now use a wheelchair."

"I am so sorry, everything is my fault," Mr. Criss muttered as he shook his head and turned to face Collin.

After spending time in recuperation, Ava was moved to her room, but no one was permitted to see her. Darsh and his family were also present.

She wanted to see Collin right away after she woke up.

Collin approached his mother in tears, took her hand in his, and kissed it since he was feeling too embarrassed to even look at her face.

Ava hardly had the strength to open her eyes, let alone speak to him. "Mom, would you please open your eyes and say something? I'm sorry. I know I'm the one who caused all of this. I'll guarantee to make things right."

After witnessing his mother in that position, he was so furious that when the nurse requested him to leave, he went without waiting in the hospital.

He began to walk in the pouring rain while contemplating how much he had harmed his family and behaved badly over the last few days. He was aware that Della was what he truly desired, but he had to pretend to be someone else in order to satisfy his family's demands. He had to stop fighting since it was ineffective.

Chapter Eight
Play Pretend

He realized this was utterly unjust, but he had to do it to save his mother's life. He walked on the road for hours while carrying for his fortune and for his destiny.

When he returned to the hospital, the nurses forbade him from entering the CCU unit. He was begging them to hold off for a moment while he went to see his mother.

Ava was dozing off and appeared quite worn out and frail. She widened her eyes and said, "I knew you would come back," as Collin went and held her hand.

Collin broke down in tears and begged for pardon. "Mom, from today, I'll only do what you and Dad wish me to do. I swear I won't dispute or argue anymore; all I want is to see you at home again."

Ava's tears were rolling very slowly. "I knew you'd make me proud; it's the only thing I want before I go."

"You won't be leaving, Mom; I'll be taking you home shortly." After kissing her forehead, he departed the hospital.

He returned immediately to his house and to the lonely spot he had created, where he wished one day, he would invite his beloved Della to join.

Olivia asked him whether he was awake when she entered his room early in the morning. He had nightmares the entire night.

Collin woke up from his couch nap and asked, "Yes, I'm awake. What's happened? How's Mum doing?"

He was given his breakfast by Olivia, who entered the room and left them on the table.

"Morning, Mum is well but remains in CCU, Dad called from the hospital, don't worry.

"I am aware of what you told your mother last night. Are you absolutely certain you are prepared to do it?"

"I know I want my mother back in this house, and I also want to avoid being so self-centered."

Olivia rushed up, kissed him, and sobbed, "I don't know what to say, Collin, thank you. If you're ready, you will propose at Mr. Aiden's house tonight.

"Why so soon?" Collin's expression abruptly changed to one of a dreamer.

"Dad believes that if we complete this task more quickly, Mom will recuperate more quickly."

"Dad obviously had to say that," Collin said while sporting a dejected expression.

"If Della is not in my life, why should I worry, who will take her place or what will happen next?" Collin asked as he walked to sit down at the table for breakfast. "I only have one goal in mind: to rescue and return my mum."

Because this was the only thing affecting their mother's health, Olivia was aware of how devastated her brother was and how much he had prepared for his marriage with Della.

As night swiftly fell, Olivia went to see how Collin was doing. She found him dressed for the occasion, but he had no soul and no grin. "Are you still certain that you want to do this? Dad is waiting outside."

"Let's go, everything is wonderful; if karma compels me to do this, then I must do it."

Collin told Olivia to wait for him outside, while he went and made a call to Della.

He told her about his mother's illness and that he had agreed to do what she asked of him, but he was not pleased with Della's response. "I'm glad you're starting to think clearly, but please don't tell anyone about our plan— otherwise, everything will go wrong. Be strong, and know that I love you."

"How can you say, you love me," yelled Collin, "then you want me to go with a different woman. What if she didn't want me to divorce her? What if she wanted to have a child?"

"We belong to each other, so please stop worrying about these things. I'm here to guide you through every stage, and I love you, baby."

Collin hurriedly ended the call and made his way to the car while wearing a dejected expression after hearing his father honking again.

Mr. Criss told him, "Let's get flowers and a huge box of chocolates on the way."

Collin walked up to the first flower shop, hastily grabbed the first bouquet of flowers he saw, and left.

Mr. Criss instructed Olivia to get down and pick something nice and costly this time at the sweetshop.

"Don't worry, sister; this family will still accept us if we arrive with nothing." While Olivia was getting out of the car, Collin told her.

"Don't be too confident, after what you did to that poor girl, I barely questioned they even allowed us in," Mr. Criss retorted.

After then, it took them twenty minutes to get to Mr. Roy's residence.

Aiden's home was stunning, and the yard, which included many flowers of various colors, appeared to be from a fairy tale, amazing sculptures and a lovely pool.

Collin could tell it was Ocean's father from the way he looked when a man stepped out to welcome them inside.

"Oh Criss, I didn't know your son was so attractive. Where did he get this look? Definite from Ava, not you!"

Mr. Aiden welcomed everyone and extended an invitation. Raya also stepped out to welcome them; Collin saw why Ocean was so fascinating as a result of her mother beauty.

They all went and sat on the sofa; everything in the house was vintage, making it feel like a museum. When Collin wondered why a girl from such a wealthy family had to work for him, he suddenly remembered the excuse he had to use to terminate her. He felt very ashamed of himself.

Raya then began inquiring about Ava's health, and Collin suddenly realized that he had made a promise to his mother and that he had to keep it.

Ocean was looking in the mirror and couldn't believe the man who had just dismissed her a few days prior had now come to propose to her.

Why did he have to break her heart, she pondered. She reasoned that perhaps he didn't want his future bride to work where he did or that he didn't want his employees to believe that they were having an illicit connection.

Although she was aware that this was what she desired—to be with Collin and wed him—she was not content, as something inside of her argued that everything she was doing was incorrect.

Her mother was astonished to see her still in her pajamas when she entered the room because she wasn't quite ready.

"Ocean, today is a significant day for you. Wasn't this what you wanted? He is currently waiting for you downstairs, what is going on with you? I knew you had feelings for him but I never told you anything."

Ocean was stumped when asked, "Mom, can I not come down? I know I desire him and that I adore him, but I don't feel quite right I know I desire him, but I barley know him, and now that he has not even apologized to me for what he did to me at work, he wants to ask me to marry him?"

"My love, if you sit here and lock yourself in your room, you won't get answer to any of your questions, therefore it's best to ask him everything," Raya remarked as she walked to sit next to Ocean and held her hand. "Additionally, there is no rush; if you decide you don't want him, simply say so; I'm confident he will understand."

"Why didn't they wait till Mrs. Ava was discharged?" Ocean asked, still unsatisfied. "What's with the hurry?"

"As you are aware, Ava's health is not stable, and she expressed a wish to witness her son marrying you; hence, they are present without her. Collin is hoping that his mother would feel better following today's proposal, Raya answered.

She then instructed Ocean to get ready immediately and head downstairs.

Ocean glanced in the mirror and watched her tears slowly flow from her eyes. She wanted Collin and they had just misunderstood one another, and she prayed he had at least once noticed how beautiful she was at the workplace.

She quickly got dressed and headed downstairs. She was staring at Collin as she descended the steps, but he failed to notice her.

Olivia just became aware of Ocean at that moment, when she stood up in front of her and dragged Collin up with her.

During their handshake, Ocean asked Collin, "Why are you here?" while gazing into his eyes.

Collin didn't have any responses, so he simply kept his head down and made an effort not to look at her at all.

Mr. Criss eventually started gushing about Ocean and how nicely her family had reared her.

"My darling, Ocean, you are aware of our friendship. Today, with your father's approval, I am here to ask you to wed my son."

Ocean's father then interjected, saying, "Criss, the times have changed, and the younger generations are entirely different. I have always given Ocean all the privileges to make a choice about her life, and in this matter, it depends on her. If she wanted to have an arranged marriage, I wouldn't stop her, nor would I encourage her."

Then, everyone was waiting for Ocean to speak, including Collin, who was nervously staring at her despite his high level of confidence that Ocean would accept.

Ocean felt a lot of pressure and was contemplating the passing of time. She was thrilled when Mr. Criss called to let her know they were on the way, but at the moment she was unable to breathe even, because she had no idea how to handle a boy like him.

She said, "It is very lovely of you to think highly of me uncle Criss, and I am pleased I am the chosen one, however regrettably I cannot be a decent wife for your son." Before hastily getting to her feet, saying, "You have to forgive me," and walking out.

Collin's expression changed when he heard Ocean say no; this was the very first time a girl had rejected him, and he was absolutely baffled.

Then, because everyone was quiet, Mr. Aiden had to give a speech, "I apologize, my friend, but I don't want to put pressure on her because she's still so young, I hope you'll understand. Since she is the only asset I have, her happiness means everything to me."

"At the end of the day, my son has injured her feelings and she has the right to reject him; it shows she genuinely cares about what is happening. However, don't forget we will not give up and I will keep coming here until she says yes to my son and accept him."

Collin was really angry to hear his father speak, and he kept thinking to himself that his father refused to accept Della, and here he was sitting and pleading this self-centered girl.

After a brief conversation, they departed Mr. Aiden's home, with the assurance that they would return.

Collin lost his patience in the car and began arguing with his father once more, saying, "Why do you have to put me down, I don't like that girl, I can't be with her, can't you see that? I'm not going to go back to that house because I've already fulfilled my vow and there is nothing else I can do."

Mr Criss lit his cigar and opened the shatter because he knew Collin was looking for something to start wrecking the evening.

"You mistreated Ocean and did something wrong, so what do you expect? I told you that she is unlike any other females you have ever met, so we need to give her time to reflect before trying again."

Collin was then instructed to visit the hospital since Ava was waiting for them.

Olivia really loved Ocean, but she knew that complimenting her would make Collin very angry, so she tried to keep quiet.

They were all prohibited from going to visit Ava because it was already pretty late. Collin was ordered to go by Mr. Criss after he had already left and returned.

Ava had lost a lot of weight in a short period of time, her eyes were scarcely opening, and she was unable to speak. Collin was devastated for his mother because she was everything to him.

When he saw his mother resting on a hospital bed and him outside the hospital battling for Della, he knew it was his fault for allowing her to get to this point.

Which one required more attention? Who was in the right and who out? He was aware that he had to stand up for his love, but not at the expense of his mother's life!

"Mom, I kept my word, but she still refused me. What else could I do to bring you happiness?"

"I want to see you smile, and I want you to enjoy. If you believe Della will give you that, then by all means, pursue her. However, if you still have any doubts in your heart, then try listening to your family."

She then began to cough, at which point the nurse entered the room and asked Collin to leave.

He was devastated, sat on the chair outside of his mother's room, and wept for her and for his bad luck because he couldn't even get a chance to say good night to his poor mother, who didn't deserve to be there. He was the one pressuring Della into this romance even though he was aware that she didn't want him.

He had to assist his mother in returning home because both Olivia and he needed her. After wiping away his emotions, he headed back to the car.

Chapter Nine
Start Another Fire

Ocean didn't get any rest the entire night since she kept wondering when Collin would return! She couldn't believe she had rejected his affection and gone her separate way.

She was displeased with herself since she hadn't even had breakfast and wasn't chatting with anyone at home.

She had planned to go for a run, hoping that would assist her to relieve her stress. When the phone rang, the housekeeper replied, "Mam, it is for you, Sir Collin wants to talk to you!"

"Who is it?" inquired Ocean, who immediately stopped and stared at her.

The maid then said, "Sir Collin wants to chat to you Mam," repeating herself.

She stepped to the front and got the phone from her before attempting to calm herself. However, her hands were shaking and she was having trouble breathing, so she had to pretend.

"Hello."

"Hello, it's Collin. I'm very sorry to have bothered you in this way, but I had to speak to you, preferably in person! If you don't mind, I'll come pick you up at five if I have a couple things to explain."

Ocean questioned whether she was speaking to the correct Collin because the Collin she knew was not the type to explain anything to anyone.

"Sure, no problem, I'm good with five."

She hurriedly said goodbye and ended the conversation. She was certain she was dreaming since the relationship between the two people seemed to be straight out of a fairy tale.

Sadly, he was unable to even glance at her in the office; not once did he smile. Even though he has been turned down, he is still pursuing her and pleading with her to meet him.

When Raya noticed Ocean was quietly contemplating something, she intervened, asking, "Ocean, are you okay, darling? Who was it?"

"Mom, don't worry, I'm fine. It was Collin."

Raya asked anxiously, "Is Ava okay?"

"Don't panic, mother, he was requesting your lovely daughter to see him this evening because he wanted to clarify himself, as I stated."

"He loves you and you adore him, it is so evident that you two were meant to be together, "Raya said as she began to cheer.

Then the housekeeper joined in on the cheering and congratulations for Ocean.

"Please stop it everyone, I just want to hear what he has to say, that's all." After that, Raya and the helpers exchanged giggling glances.

"I am your mother, and I am not blind. If you didn't desire him, you would not have agreed to go out with him. Sit in the vehicle and quietly hear to his narrative."

Ocean was aware that she had to accept it because there was no other possibility.

***

She had prepared for Collin's arrival and was waiting for him. She had been practicing her speeches and smiles, but she was unsure about how to act.

She reasoned that she had many relationships in her life, so why did she feel differently about this one? Why did she have to fall in love with someone so unknowledgeable?

Ocean paused a little while before opening after Collin rang the doorbell. He continued to wait outside for her while acting like a gentleman by opening the car door.

He asked her where she would like to go after getting in. "Anywhere close by would be preferable."

"All well then. I am aware of a nearby location with great coffee."

Both of them were silent in the car as Ocean inadvertently glanced his way while inhaling his perfume.

Both customers in the coffee shop placed their orders.

Collin wasn't sure where to begin as he admired Ocean's remarkable beauty; she was truly a Spanish gorgeousness. He was in love with Della even though she was nothing like everyone else.

He knew that if Della had not entered his life, Ocean would have been the ideal match for him, but at this point, Della had already stolen his heart, and he could do nothing but play his part.

"I'm not sure where to begin or what to say in light of what I've already done. I want to apologize for whatever I did to offend you, and I kindly ask for your forgiveness because I was under a lot of stress at the time."

"So, you'll terminate a staff member every time you're under pressure at work?"

She was correct, and Collin knew it as he stared at her, but he still needed to put things right. "No, you were the center of attention, and I felt envious since I couldn't see anyone higher than me. I apologize."

"I wasn't upset, but I was shocked and disappointed because I was hoping for promotions. It's fine, I don't want to talk about it, and I've forgotten it."

After drinking a little of his coffee, Collin said, "I came today here to personally address the issues between us and request you marrying me. I need to obtain your yes today because of my mother!"

Collin realized he made a mistake when Ocean's expression altered. "So, either you want to marry me or your mother is begging you to?"

Collin was felling terrible because he had to act as a lover or as someone who is completely adoring her, to make her believe him.

"Please don't get me wrong, obviously I'm the one who's interested, but my family also likes you so much and they're also asking me to not waste time since a girl with your personality and appearance might easily attract many guys and I'll miss my chance."

He couldn't look into Ocean's eyes while speaking since he was feeling bad for ruining this girl's life. He knew well that he would never make her happy, but he had no choice but to do this.

To avoid losing his passion, Collin had to fabricate lies after lies in order to respond to her inquiries.

"You are not a typical lady; you are lovely, intelligent, perceptive, and from a respectable society. Who would not desire this?

"Would you be my wife?" he asked again after noticing Ocean was smiling a little.

"I'd appreciate some time to reflect."

"My mother is waiting, so please."

"So, what will happen when I say no?" Ocean asked while grinning.

"I'll keep coming until you accept my offer of you as a partner."

After hearing the final words, Ocean could no longer hold on. She knew she was in love with him, so why bother pestering him any longer? Just say yes and finish it.

"If my family has approved, I'm fine with it."

Everyone in the coffee shop praised both of them as Collin clapped his hands and exclaimed with excitement.

They immediately paid the bill and left the place, both of them quiet in the car. Ocean was glad, but she wasn't entirely sure she had made the right decision since he still felt like a complete stranger to her. He was a very mysterious man, which made her like him even more.

Soon before saying good-bye, Collin informed her that they will visit to make arrangements for the engagement day.

As Raya awaited Ocean's arrival in the hallway, she was asking plenty of questions. "So, tell me, how it went?"

Ocean struggled mightily to keep her emotions under control as she said, "Mom, I responded by saying yes."

Raya began to shout in joy, and the housemaids immediately rushed to see what was wrong. Mr. Aiden was astounded to see that his daughter had accepted Collin's proposal.

"How quickly you agreed, weren't you the one who claimed you didn't really understand Collin's characteristics and needed more time to do so?" Aiden enquired.

"We too didn't know each other adequately and we were connected by a buddy," Raya said in response this time. "Have you forgotten that you asked me to marry you less than one month."

Ocean interrupted her mother's laughter by saying, "Dad, I adore him and I can't conceal it, I know it seems ridiculous, but I was even amazed by my own acceptance of his proposal. I am content because you were the one to say that I should make the final decision, so I did. Hopefully, I won't be sorry!"

Everyone seemed to be happy with the idea, but Ocean still couldn't figure out what was missing. She was still terrified inside, but she knew she loved him and that these kinds of feelings would pass quickly.

Chapter Ten
For Better or Worse

Collin felt ashamed of what he had been doing and was really exhausted. Ocean was falling for him, and he could tell by the look of love in her eyes, it was so wrong, he had to quit and promise to stop hurting Ocean.

When he broke the news to his mother in the hospital, she grinned and appeared pleased. "Mom, if she discovers out about my connection with Della, she'll find out I have a wife."

"Don't be ridiculous; everyone has a past, and you are one of them. I'm sure Ocean had relationships before you, but she's chosen to accept them and go on. Why can't you accomplish the same?"

Collin didn't want to disagree. Ava had asked him to start making plans for a large wedding as by then she would undoubtedly be released from the hospital.

He tried to phone Della while he was on the way to let her know what had happened, but as usual, she did not pick up. He then went to Della's house, but it was vacant.

He was in utter disbelief—how could Della move without even telling him!

He was wondering why he had to put up with all of these problems in his life the entire trip home. His loneliness and disappointment led him to consider committing suicide. Sadly, his mother and Olivia thoughts prevented him from even doing that.

***

At Mr. Aiden's home, almost everyone was gathered. Olivia, Mr. Criss, and Collin were present along with Darsh and his family.

Everyone was chatting and sharing ideas regarding the venue for the wedding party, but Collin was regretfully sitting in a corner by himself, paying no attention to anything.

Raya went to see why Ocean wasn't joining the others and found her still in her room. "Ocean," she said. "Dear Love Does something seem off?"

Ocean was already wearing a green silky dress and a red lipstick. Her beautiful black hair was kept in place.

"Something is wrong; else, I would not feel this way."

"It's still not too late, you can say no to anything and end it, even if in the future you felt he wasn't the one, simply leave him," Ava whispered as she drew nearer and took her hand. "Force does not exist."

After speaking with her mother, she felt better, and they both joined the crowd.

Because of her beauty and the fact that he was about to marry her, Collin could not help but stare at her. He began to feel a connection to her.

Even in his own thoughts, however, he knew that he couldn't do that since he needed to find Della, his missing wife. She was the one who encouraged him to pretend, so he reasoned that even if she finds out about the party tonight, she simply would not care.

Ocean was directed to a seat next to Collin. She saw Collin's face and thought to herself, *Why is he so unhappy? What is he trying to hide?* She pondered the possibility that he was experiencing the same emotions as she was.

The decision was made to proceed with the engagement after two weeks, and Mr. Aiden was the only one who objected to the chosen date.

"Come on, Aiden, two weeks or a month doesn't matter; if these two are in love, there's no reason to keep pushing back their engagement date."

Ocean received a diamond ring from Collin as a token of their commitment, and she and her family also received several gifts. Everyone pretended to be joyful and having a great time.

As soon as Collin excused himself from the crowd and left for the garden to take a break, Darsh instantly followed.

After they had left together, Ocean glanced at her mother with amazement, but Raya wanted to escape her and her uncertainties, so she kept herself occupied.

"Collin brother, stop hurrying, where are you going?"

Collin was so angry that he wanted to run away. "I can't breathe there; why am I doing all of this? Can't you see that Ocean is being persecuted because of me? Her face is so innocent."

"I understand, but try to see the bright side. She will soon become your wife, and everything will be forgotten. As a result, stop hurting yourself; you have already gone so far."

"You're just as ignorant as the rest of them, nobody even asks the groom why he's sad or why he keeps avoiding talks and showing no indication of having any plans of his own for the ceremony."

Darsh tried to change the subject by saying, "Collin, I realize this is not the proper time but I have to inform you about something, as for the last few days you are not coming to office either." Darsh knew that by disputing with him he would not get anything.

"Is there an issue with my absence at the office," Collin asked, looking at him.

"Everything is OKAY, but I want to talk to you about me and Olivia tonight. I know it was a plan to talk to our mothers and then they would get our fathers involved, however it didn't work with me."

Collin's expression changed, and he realized that he had completely forgotten about that despite his sister's vow that he would assist her.

"I'm ashamed, although I tried, but my father even spanked me for considering marrying Olivia, saying that it would be foolish of me to betray their trust by falling in love with her.

"So, as you can see, it's not only you who has to seem joyful," Darsh said as he went and sat down on one of the benches in the Garden.

"Does Olivia know?" he said as Collin followed suit.

"She cried so hard when I informed her a few days ago, but she also decided not to discuss it because of your mother's illness."

"Keep running with her, get married in another country," Collin murmured while keeping his hand on Darsh's shoulder. "They have already destroyed my life, so you two still have a chance. You two shouldn't stay in this disaster."

"We can't save her from death and then kill her by fleeing again, Collin. I'm the only kid of my family, and your mother needs Olivia."

"We accepted that we would each marry another person and carry on with our lives. It is not simple, but it is doable. I'm aware that none of us will ever be content, yet this is our lot in life and the world is currently happy this way."

He then got to his feet and raised Collin's hands. "I wanted to let you know that we understand your suffering and that we are here for you. The only thing that separates us from you, though, is that we have learned to smile while we are grieving."

Collin made numerous attempts to get in touch with Della after that night but her phone was always off. He was quite disappointed in her because she was the one who coerced him into doing all of these things, and when she suddenly vanished, Collin knew she was out partying without considering what was going on with him.

***

Everyone was busy getting ready for the wedding ceremony, so the two weeks flew by. It was decided by Criss and Aiden to have their children's wedding at the modest temple outside of town where they had their own many years prior.

Additionally, everyone who attended the wedding was invited to a neighboring hotel for a lunch with the couple.

Both families opted to keep it more private and avoid inviting many people.

With the money they were spending, they were able to complete everything swiftly thanks to the services of a wedding planner.

When the big day finally arrived, the wedding coordinator instructed Collin to go and pick up Ocean and travel to a stunning location for photo shoots.

It was difficult for Collin to grin in any photographs, and Ocean was depressed as well, crying unnoticed. The duo was acting extremely tense.

Even though Ava was in a wheelchair, she was dressed and thrilled to attend her son's engagement party. Collin was delighted to see her giggling, clapping, and beaming with joy. She welcomed him and Ocean into her presence, blessed their relationship, and sent them only positive vibes.

Collin was required to dance with his engaged partner despite being unaware of this aspect of the plan; he was unable to object because Ocean was standing exactly next to him.

It was Ed Sheeran's song, "Perfect," and as he took Ocean's hand for the first time, he felt fire spread throughout his body. He had to keep her close to him since Ocean was reluctant to look into his eyes, and he was, in fact, staring at her.

The crowd was stunned by how these two were hugging each other at that precise moment and by the amazing dance they were performing. It appeared as though they were rehearsing together every day.

Ocean was wishing she could stop time so she could stare directly into Collin's eyes and declare her undying love for him. Despite knowing she wouldn't receive the same love in return from Collin, Ocean was still smitten with Collin.

Collin and his family also left quite quickly as the celebration ended.

Ocean spent the entire evening singing and dancing with her mother, believing that Collin was the prince from a fairy tale. With these same beliefs, Ocean went to bed.

Chapter Eleven
Having Nothing Left

As the days went by, Ocean's existence become progressively less enjoyable. She was having trouble with the odd relationship. She barely spoke to Collin for a little under three hours over the last two months of their engagement, and she only saw him 2–3 times; those occasions were with his family, not just by himself.

Ocean was not pleased with the large ceremony held at Mr. Criss' house to celebrate Collin's birthday. She was experiencing a dreadful sense that something terrible was about to occur. She was deciding that tonight would be the night she finally received all of the answers to her inquiries.

With all those lights around it, the garden looked fantastic and the home was exquisitely decorated.

For Collin's birthday, a fantastic band was invited to perform. Ava was as content as ever and wouldn't let Ocean sit anywhere else but next to her.

Olivia had lost her personality and was now just following the rules like the rest.

Ocean was requested to hurry up and call the birthday boy from his room, but she had no idea where to go. She then invited Olivia to join her.

The door to Collin's room was open, so they both entered. Collin was sitting in the dark with a voice recorder in one hand—the same one he had hidden in Della's room a few months earlier—and some photographs in the other.

He asked Olivia to turn off the lights and leave the room because he wanted some time alone with Ocean.

Ocean was shocked that he was asking for her for the first time! As Olivia turned around and walked away, she pleaded with him to hurry up because everyone was waiting for him.

"You were the one who was often asking me what was behind my sad eyes, therefore it is best you check it yourself," he said, opening the table lamp beside him. His eyes were red, his face was so frightening, and his hair was disheveled. He requested Ocean to sit.

Then he handed her a couple images that he had in his possession. One of the pictures was of Della wearing her wedding dress, and the groom was Della's best friend Michell. Ocean was unaware of what was taking place.

"This is Della, the woman I was going to marry, but she is now marrying someone else. She has been the love of my life; these pictures have been preserved on my table by my father so I can stop loving her and start adoring you in her place."

Ocean broke down in tears since she hadn't anticipated such a stern introduction from him.

He requested her to stop sobbing since it was making him uncomfortable. "Now, kindly take note of this: I had concealed the voice recorder at Della's home a few days prior to my mother's hospitalization, and regrettably today, I remembered to hear it."

Then he played it without even glancing at Ocean.

It was obvious that voice belonged to Mr. Criss. "You need to quit your nonsense, Della. I committed a mistake years ago, so why should my son be compelled to pay for it now?"

Ocean was still perplexed and unsure of what was going on when Collin paused the recording to try and clarify: "That day after I left, my father was gone to her apartment. I knew he was following me, which is why I came up with this plan to record their discussion. Please listen carefully."

Della was laughing as he played it again, and after a little while she reacted, "You abandoned me. My mother repeatedly tried to get in touch with you, but you were not even concerned to recognize your own guilt and attempt to at least financially take care of us."

"We've been through this before, and as I told you, I paid her, but she was addicted and spent all of it on drugs."

"The day mom died, they seized me; I was left without parents or support; the family who fostered me used me unfairly. I eventually ended up working in a casino, dealing drugs, performing on stage, and doing much worse. Where were you, my dear father? I was your child too, just like Collin and Olivia, but you abandoned me."

"Stop your dishonest behavior; you made Collin fall in love with you; what have you turned into? Collin is your brother, and you are animal. What are you expecting from me?"

"You were prepared to kill me so I wouldn't disturb you or your family, but today you are pleading for your son's life back from me. I was also your daughter."

"Please Della, you have caused enough harm. I will pay you everything you demand, register one of my businesses in your name, and give you the largest property I have ever owned. Simply leave Collin alone; he is a good man."

Collin had Ocean's whole attention when he was sobbing like a young boy and no longer acting like the serious boss and strong guy she had known. He appeared to be extremely confused and afraid.

She then learned that Della had been offered a sizable sum of money, which she accepted. In addition, she had to pretend to be married and provide some images of herself with her new spouse. She also had to depart right away and never look back.

Ocean was silent this time, not crying anymore, and she was just staring at her distraught fiancé, wondering at this very moment, what should she do?

Why was she at the center of everything and why did Collin choose her to be his wife? For a lady like her, accepting that her fiancé had a history with another female and was over it was quite simple, but this situation was unique!

He convinced her that he was in love with her, which was harsh and cruel. Now that he's opening up, he claims that everything was planned. She wondered which scheme in existence would enable individuals to profit from human emotions.

She dried her tears and stood up. As she looked steely at Collin, she left the room. However, not even once did Collin attempt to stop her.

Everyone in the garden was waiting for them to appear together, but as usual, only Ocean was there.

"How is your fiancée doing? The cake is melting, and we're sick of waiting here. You had one duty," said Olivia.

"I never agreed to any responsibilities," Ocean remarked as he turned to face her.

Then, without even glancing at her own parents, she moved toward the gate and stepped outside.

Criss and Ava were perplexed as Raya and Aiden chased after her, and they wondered what had transpired between them to cause this.

Even though her parents were calling her, Ocean was walking on the sidewalk and was unable to hear them. Ocean was in a parallel reality when Raya went to hold her hand; it was frozen. "Ocean, what is happening, please tell me. Do you want us to drive you home?" she enquired.

"Mom, I am extremely weary; I need to rest," Ocean said as she turned to face her mother in the middle of the street.

She was completely silent as they drove her home; perhaps she was still attempting to comprehend what had happened to her.

Once they arrived at their house, Ocean walked to her room, turned off the lights, and begged her parents to go so she could sleep. She did this without even changing clothes!

Her parents were really concerned about what had unexpectedly happened.

"Why can't we ask her what's going on? We must take action in response to this! Maybe we can assist," added Aiden.

"You know her very well; when she's unhappy, she won't talk. We need to give her some time. She'll tell us everything," Raya responded to him.

The following day, when there was still no word from Ocean, it was around lunchtime. Raya went to her room and said, "Ocean, you need to eat something. If you don't inform us of what happened, your father will contact Collin's folks and request that they explain what he has done to you."

She panicked when she heard Collin's name and urged her mother not to contact him; Mr. Aiden was also present.

She said, "Just don't call anybody, I will tell you," and then she started crying.

"Collin was compelled to engage me by his family since he was already engaged to another woman and they had plans to marry.

"He was punishing himself for what had happened to his mother, and he wanted to do something for her, which is why they were all pursuing me. I was the target of their pursuit." Then she gave a detailed explanation of everything, including the voice recorder, images, and Della.

Since so many details were revealed at once, Aiden and Raya were stunned for a moment. Ocean broke the awkward silence between them by saying, "I don't really care about what Collin is going through right now. Why me? They could have selected anybody else, but they pursued me simply because I was so accessible and easy to persuade.

She was angry and depressed by her failure. Mr. Aiden disapproved of what she was doing and told her, "I offered you a choice. First you said no to him and, unexpectedly he planned to meet you for coffee and, within half an hour you were the person who stated yes to him and decided to stay with him."

Ocean felt so angry with herself for her foolishness even though she knew her dad was correct.

"These are all experiences. I know it came to you in a hard way, but at least you aren't married to him, and it's just a ring, so you can return it whenever you want. None of them are your mistakes, so stop blaming yourself. I'll make arrangements for us to return to Spain with the help of your father."

Aiden nodded and agreed with Raya's statement before the two of them left the room.

Ocean was still in shock, but she knew she still loved him and that if she didn't stay with him, she wouldn't live. She needed to understand that Collin was seeing someone else, though.

Who was the girl, though? She inquired. She now felt awful for Collin because he had been in love with his sister the entire time! God only knows what more they had accomplished as a couple! He had a plan to even get married to her! He was in a horrible mood. Neither she nor he deserved such misfortune!

Chapter Twelve
Still Breathing

After a few days, Mr. Criss eventually appeared at Ocean's home. Even though Aiden didn't want to, he insisted on coming in anyway.

Ocean has been in bed for days with a high fever, unable to eat, and receiving care from a nurse who has been at her bed the entire time.

"I'm here to apologize; this is entirely my responsibility; I did this. I refrained from commenting on Collin's relationship because it was a complete disaster. I was aware that Ocean had informed you of what Collin had said to her. I regret it. I am absolutely lost. I hoped I could accept Della as my daughter as I never anticipated how she would get back at me."

Still displeased, Mr. Aiden said, "Since that terrible night, my daughter has remained in bed; she is sickly and still reeling from the experience. Why did you seek us out? You were well aware of how precious my only child is to her mother and me."

"I apologize; feel free to place all the blame on me; nevertheless, Collin is currently in a bad condition, and Ava has returned to the hospital, so I have come to you for assistance. My wife and son are leaving me."

"I don't know what to do," he said while expressing his distress.

"You must aid me. Since I was aware of how you had reared her, I came for your daughter because I believed she could save Collin. She shines brightly like a diamond.

"I never intended to harm her or Collin at all. I wanted Collin to see Ocean's genuine love and let go of the past as I had no idea he had a voice recorder hidden in that house."

"I know I've done wrong, but I can't let my family down since I should be the one being admitted to the hospital, not my wife. My family no longer wants me."

Ocean swiftly ran downstairs to visit Mr. Criss after overhearing their talk upstairs.

She was being helped to walk by the nurse, but she was so frail and hardly had any balance that she was still curious as to what was going on.

Mr. Criss was shocked to see Ocean in such bad shape; she was so skinny and bony that he couldn't believe it.

Aiden got up to help his daughter, and she was asked to take a seat next to him.

"I am ashamed, I never intended to harm you, God is my testimony. I wanted to heal my son, and the day I met you in my workplace, I decided to include you into my family."

Then Criss spoke again, saying, "I came here today to solicit help from you and your father but after seeing you in this state, I feel your father was right, regrettably you are not fine at all." Ocean was unable to speak but only nodded her head.

"Is Collin OKAY?" Ocean questioned.

"No Ocean, Collin is sick. That day after you left, he took the car and went away, while we didn't know what was going on. He had an accident, and then for three days he was in a comma.

"And thereafter, he was released from the hospital and sent home, but he had lost his short memory. He keeps hurting himself while talking rubbish. Ava isn't here, and Olivia is constantly in the hospital with her mother."

Occan broke down in tears after learning what had happened to Collin since she felt so awful. He was her first love, yet she wasn't even there to care for him.

"I'm sorry this happened, but I can't let my daughter become involved with you and your family issues again. We're leaving the country in two days, and I don't want Ocean to suffer any further harm."

Then Mr. Aiden immediately requested that the nurse come and accompany Ocean while she returned to her room.

When Ocean was returned to her room, Collin remained on her mind. She continued to be in love with him and could not let go of him. Ocean felt what had happened to her was wrong, but she also understood that Collin didn't mean to harm her and that what had happened to him was equally unfair.

Hopeless and unable to do anything else to support his family, Criss left that day. His only choice was to go to Ocean.

Ocean was restless; now that she was aware of what had happened to Collin, she was feeling guilty. She needed to make a choice, but she wasn't sure what would occur in the future.

Raya had just gotten home and had only found that Criss had visited earlier. Ocean asked her parents to come to her room.

Ocean made an effort to act as though she was feeling better and had already taken a shower and eaten.

"I want you two to support me in this decision, therefore I've invited you to come here." Raya stared at Aiden's face in horror, unsure of what might transpire. She looked at her daughter while holding her husband's hand.

"I want to go back to Collin. I understand that they lied to us, but I still care about him, since what happened to both of us was unfair. I'm in a different circumstance right now because Collin needs me. I must accompany him."

"They have fooled us, my love, that boy doesn't even want you, therefore this is not your concern," Raya said as she went and sat on Ocean's bed. "How can you claim you want to go back after he took advantage of your emotions?"

"Mum, I am the one who is wanting Collin; I am the one who desires to be with him; I want to give myself a chance; I want to give our partnership another shot. I am aware that this sounds foolish, yet I can't help but feel this way. Don't stop me, Mom, please. I need to see him."

Raya was in tears. She pleaded with Aiden, "Please say something, she's gone crazy."

"Your mother is right; this family might harm you again. They're in a lot of trouble. You can't cure anything. You have to understand us. We're here to protect you from the pain that's going to come to you in the future."

"I'm not a teenager, I know what happened, but I can't leave Collin alone. His narrative finished with that wicked woman, but our book is still open, and I need to have an ending to this story, whether it be joyful or sad. Since you two are the only family I have, I want you to be there for me no matter what."

Ocean's parents couldn't say anything since they had to accept her decision and understood that if they persisted any further, things would get worse. Ocean and Raya cried while being held close.

"Don't worry, Mom, I'll make it, and I'll assure you that nothing bad will happen to me because I want to spend time with him. I'm powerless to quit."

Then she asked her father to tell Criss she would be joining them tomorrow.

***

Ocean was prepared the following day and ready to go when her father-in-law arrived with the assistance of the nurse.

Ocean's family was not happy at all, and Raya was so anxious that day that she kept pleading with Aiden to persuade Ocean to reconsider and stay. However, it appeared like nothing was working.

Ocean hugged her mom and reassured her once more that nothing to worry about. "I had many dreams for your wedding day and the day you would leave us and move into your husband's home, but this was not in my plan."

"It was not in my plan, either, Mom, but this is what has to happen; therefore, I must accept it."

Aiden arrived to assist her daughter in loading her suitcase into the car, and he was not pleased either.

"I know I've always backed you in any choice you've taken, but this is pure suicide. I have a horrible feeling about it. Still, you have the option to leave and control your life!"

Ocean was also experiencing fear, but she had to be brave since she needed Collin and any hesitation would have made her decide not to go.

She gave her father a big hug and reassured him that everything would be okay. They could come and see her, and she would keep in touch with them and inform them on her condition.

Mr. Criss expressed his gratitude to Aiden and Raya for letting Ocean assist his family as he was in tears and overjoyed to see Ocean.

Ocean waved at her parents as she prayed for a positive outcome as she sat in the car. Criss kept praising her and apologizing for getting her into this difficulty along the way, but Ocean was too sleepy to hear any of it. Instead, she closed her eyes and dozed out.

Ocean was expected at home, so Olivia walked to the front to greet and kiss her. "My love, you've lost a lot of weight. Since my family is going through a horrible trauma, I had to take care of them. I apologize if I didn't call you or come to visit you."

"I am aware of your condition and I have no expectations."

"Collin is in his room; I know you can't wait to see him. His cognitive impairment is not severe. He has undergone significant change, is still hurt, is taking numerous medications as a result of the accident, and is not at all stable.

He has lost his short-term memory, so if he doesn't recognize you, please accept my apologies. Although there is absolutely no guarantee, doctors are hopeful that his memory may someday return."

She then held Ocean's hand and assisted her as she climbed the stairs to visit Collin. Collin was not in his bed when they entered the room; instead, he was perched in his armchair, gazing out the window. The bandages on his head were still there.

"Collin, you cannot believe who has come to visit you!" Olivia yelled as she approached him. "Ocean is here; please come and meet her. She has decided to be with us."

In order to have a better look at Ocean, Collin got up and walked up to her. When he was almost next to her, he stopped and said, "You are extremely late, why did you come back, after all what you have done to me! Tell me, Della, why you are here."

Ocean and Olivia exchanged shocked glances as they both tried to process what Collin was saying.

"This is Ocean, your fiancé," Olivia stated as she walked forward. "She is here to look after you!"

"Do you realize how much I have gone through?" he continued, seemingly not hearing anything. "I had to hire a ton of agents to find you! How many nights and days I suffered for you!"

Then he grabbed Ocean's hand and led her away. Collin kept one bedroom always locked and forbade anybody from entering, not even his family, as it was designated "honey moon Chalet" on the door.

Ocean turned to glance behind her and noticed Olivia had remained in place, her hand hurting from Collin's tight grip. Collin then opened the door, allowing the two of them to enter.

Everything in the room was made of wood and had a classic design. There was a fountain in the center of the area, and the walls were tastefully painted. It was a lovely place with trees around and the bedroom tucked away amongst the jungle. It was breathtaking how the colors blended together.

"You see, Della, this is what I promised you. Look in this nook, all your portraits are there; it is all you had hoped for. To sketch them, I've enlisted the help of one of the best artists in the area."

Ocean could see Della's smiling images and knew she was still the victor.

She yanked her hand away from him and began to sob. She was trembling and in disbelief that all of this had been done for a lady who had injured him.

She had intended to leave the room, but Collin drew near and took hold of her hand once again, holding it close to his chest while he murmured, "Can you feel my heart beats? Please, Della, don't ever leave me again. I love you."

Ocean pulled her hand away from his grasp and left the room since she wasn't ready to be there any longer. This time, Oliva accompanied her to the garden, however before she approached the gate, Olivia urged her to pause and rest for a moment without leaving.

She advised her to take a seat on the bench and requested the housemaid to bring Ocean a glass of water.

"The actions of my father many years ago have cursed my family. My mother is in the hospital, my brother has lost his memory, and I had to sacrifice my love and my life."

Then she said, "First time, my father and brother tricked you to bring you here, but this time, knowing everything, still you made the choice to come and be with Collin." At this, Ocean looked up to hear better. "Why? What were you actually considering? What do you expect from this dysfunctional family?

"I'm not sure if Collin has ever spoken to you about me and Darsh, but we are in love and they told us it was forbidden to fall in love with your cousin, so they dismissed us.

"Collin has given Della his heart and fallen in love with his own sister! Many years ago, my father left his wife and children behind only to wed my mother, the daughter of a wealthy person. Look at us, please. We are in disarray. Despite our great wealth and power, we are unable to help ourselves."

Ocean was thinking all this time that she was the unfortunate one that her love had ended up this way since she could see through Olivia's eyes every horrible moment she had to endure. However, after taking a closer look at Olivia and her family, she began to feel as though the difficulties she was experiencing were minor when compared to Olivia's.

"I believe that we are the same age. I am aware that you are trapped in a relationship from which there is no hope for you to escape. I too was in love for a long time before deciding to move on. Even after what Collin did to you in the office, you nevertheless wanted to be with him because you loved him, even though you hardly knew him."

"I don't know why I'm here," said Ocean. "Yes, you are correct. However, I chose to stay because your brother's charm won over my heart. I loved him despite the fact that he fired me, and I have loved him for the past few days despite knowing about his background. However, this is just too much for me to handle."

"We can't compel him to recall what occurred before you; you have to understand what happened to him. He must wish to return to his usual life, according to the doctors. He won't respond to our pressure. In addition to not knowing where my mother is, he also refuses to see my father. Please rethink his demands, and if you are unable to accept them, I will grant you full permission to go."

Ocean broke down in tears once again, knowing deep down that she still loved him but that it was wrong to decide to leave him at this time. She was unsure of her intentions. She noticed Collin staring at them out of his window. She thought that the only thing that could assist her was for her to follow her heart.

Even though she was aware that loving Collin was toxic, she was nevertheless willing to accept it.

Chapter Thirteen
In the Dark

The following morning, Ocean awoke early and realized she was in Collin's home.

She had made a commitment to herself the previous evening to stay and begin taking care of Collin so that he might get better. She wanted to be courageous and stop hiding from life's challenges. She aimed to show to herself and to others that life is about accepting and forgiving.

The house was eerily quiet, as if no one had ever lived there, so she hurriedly leapt out of bed and left her room. The housekeepers were putting breakfast together as she entered the kitchen.

She requested that she be the one to take Collin's breakfast to his room from one of them who was in charge of his special diet meals.

In Collin's absence, Mr. Criss went to his office to take care of business while Olivia spent the night with her mother in the hospital.

She brought Collin's breakfast upstairs, but she realized he wasn't there when she looked. She also noticed that the door to the other room, which Collin had shown her yesterday, was open. Knowing that Collin had spent the previous night in that room, she almost felt depressed once more, but she restrained herself.

When she entered the room, Collin was lying on the bed, shirtless. She felt the need to look, so she attempted to cough to alert him to her presence.

After swiftly turning to face her and covering his body with a blanket, Collin heard Ocean say good morning and asked her to leave the meal on the table.

"I haven't seen you here before, what is your name?" he questioned her after asking her to turn in a different way so he could dress.

"My name is Ocean, and I will be your nurse starting today." Ocean was startled because he had a very different personality than she remembered him from yesterday.

"Who said I needed a nurse? I'm in perfect health, and this is just another scheme my father has come up with to get me a lovely nurse so I can spend all my time with her and entirely forget about my dear Della."

Ocean reacted angrily to Collin's mention of Della and said, "If I may recall you had an accident and you have to be monitored until a particular day and you should use your medicine according to the schedule advised by your physicians."

"Please, Ms. Ocean, tell my dad that I don't need his sympathy and that I am capable of taking care of myself. In fact, I want to go to work today and am aware of my little injury. Please leave my room right away; I do not want a nurse."

Ocean noticed Collin's eyes as she was walking away and realized they were familiar to her. She only had to think back to the times she had worked with him when he had been rude and arrogant and when they had been coworkers. In order to ensure that he had taken his medication, she left the room and sat in the waiting area.

While eating his breakfast, Collin was thinking about Ocean, what a stunning woman she is, and how his father brought her into their world to ruin his peace of mind. He knew Ocean's face was sufficiently familiar, but he was unable to recall where he had previously seen her.

He intended to visit Della's house first thing today and ask her to get ready for their impending wedding, which will take place next week in a far-off location where they will begin their new life together.

After getting dressed, he left the room and discovered Ocean seated in the hallway. "Dear Ms. Ocean, I don't wish to have a nurse, and I'll make sure you get your entire month's pay before you go today," he said. He then departed.

Ocean had to make up a story since she didn't wish Collin's family to find out that their son doesn't even welcome her as his caregiver. "I need this job. Also, I am dependent on it, so let's make a bargain. I'll stay out of your business and appear to be your nurse, and you assume that you are satisfied with your nursing assistant."

Collin noticed that she was sad and felt bad about rejecting her once more. "I agree, but keep in mind that you shouldn't meddle with my work, and I'll guarantee to lend you some money as well. Where do you sleep, by the way?"

After wiping away her tears, Ocean said, "There is room next to your honey moon suite, I stay there."

She was really attractive, and he knew she was familiar with her face, but he still couldn't recall where he had seen her. As he turned to go, he turned around to take one last look at her.

Ocean was relieved that she could at least remain in one spot with him. Since she had no plans for the remainder of the day, she decided to go to her room and begin writing in her diary.

It took her some time to write after she made the decision to visit Collin's honey moon suite as she was feeling so angry of Della for getting so much affection when she didn't even deserve it and herself for being so desperate for Collin's love and respect.

She was looking at Della's portrait and thought that she looked a lot like Collin; she was astonished that Collin hadn't noticed.

She stayed in the room for a while before leaving it to discover Olivia waiting for her. She attempted to justify her absence by stating that she was at Collin's honey moon suite, but Olivia refused to hear it.

"Don't fear, Ocean, I won't say anything, but I don't think going to that room is helpful. We kept it open because of Collin; my father wanted to dismantle the room in the past, but the physicians prevented him from doing so. When he must release her, they claimed he should make the decision."

Ocean shaken her head to indicate that she understood what Olivia was saying. Olivia then invited Ocean to join her for breakfast in the garden, so they both headed there. It took them some time to finish their meal.

Olivia then tried to lighten the mood by saying, "Do you know my father and mother are cousins? Their family believed they had to keep their money to themselves only, so my mother was the girl of one of the highest earning businessmen in the town and my father was the son of the 2nd wealthiest man in the city, so they had to get married.

"Their first two kids would die in a few months due to a genetic condition. After Collin was arrived, my father made a big deal about doing away with the tradition of relatives getting married and won't permit any of their children to follow this rule.

"It's interesting that his own daughter will be in love with his brother's son, after all of these years. They were all compelled into these kinds of marriages, while I and Darsh are different since we love one other."

"I know your father won't refuse my requests, so do you want me to speak with him about you two?" Ocean enquired.

"I wish it were that easy, but Darsh doesn't want to continue. After all that has occurred to my family, he doesn't want to be the cause of any more suffering, and I believe that he is right.

"The reason I told you this was to show you how easily time can rewrite the policy, and in your scenario, it has done so. I think now is the best time even though Della is our sister and Collin will shortly notice who she is. Additionally, your love is sincere, and I'm confident that it will compel him to adore you."

Ocean was wishing it was as simple as Olivia was making it sound; after all, Collin didn't even want her to be his nurse, let alone his lover!

The two then got work tending to their gardens; Ocean began instructing Olivia because she was quite knowledgeable about the vegetation.

"When will Ava return home?" Ocean enquired.

"Honestly, she chooses to stay there. After learning the truth about my dad and his daughter, she did not want to continue her marriage with him. On the other hand, seeing Collin in that state is making her more concerned."

Ocean was at a loss for words as to how to make Olivia feel better. This time, Olivia asked, "I am so envious of your family, they are open minded and let you to do what feel. We are always under our parents' control here, so normally stuff like this won't happen!"

"I have grown up in a foreign culture, therefore my parents definitely will act different, but I am very happy of them because no matter what, they have been supportive." Ocean grinned as she struggled to get her hands clean.

When Olivia noticed that she had been in the garden for three hours, she sprang to her feet and said, "I can't believe it. I have to go to the hospital. The doctor is going to do some tests on my mom, and he wants me to be there too. I'm sorry, but I must go, my dear."

Ocean found herself alone once more and began to wonder about Collin and where he might have gone. She was afraid that if he came back, he might not recognize her and she would have to start playing a fresh role, so she practiced her dialogue in anticipation of his arrival.

While she was in the garden, she made the decision to record every event that was taking place in her diary so that when Collin returned to normalcy, she could let him read it and learn what had been occurring all this time.

Around six o'clock in the evening, Olivia and Mr. Criss returned home, having Ava with them. She was pleasantly delighted to find Ava there and went to give her a hug while expressing her happiness and astonishment.

"After doing the necessary tests on my mother, the physicians declared that she is stable and is now able to go home. She was excited to see the couples reuniting after I told her about you and Collin." While speaking, Olivia gave Ocean a quick blink.

After giving Ocean a bear hug, Mr. Criss requested her to join him for a cup of tea. "I haven't had a chance to talk to you in the last two days because I've been so busy. How have you been doing? Have your parents been contacted?"

"I had phoned my mother yesterday, and concerning Collin, sadly he does not recognize me, the first time he was believing I am Della, and the second day, he assumed I am his caregiver and you have hired me to keep him occupied so he won't be thinking about Della while he is at home recovering!"

"I am sorry you are going through all of this. This is not your battle, and I am the one who caused it all. However, I am unsure of how long it will take for him to get back to normal. Please give him more time; I have no doubt that he will recover."

Ocean grinned at him before apologizing and leaving to assist her mother-in-law with the settlement.

She was hesitant to talk about Collin and herself because she was aware that they had been both involved in an unhappy partner.

They both left the room and let Ava rest after assisting Olivia in calming her mother. Ocean decided to question Olivia if she had made the correct decision to bring Ava home in this state because she was still in shock over her return from the hospital.

Olivia said, wiping away her tears, "I know you're shocked, but me and Dad had to do that because tragically, her heart wasn't functioning properly and having another surgery wasn't recommended.

"Dad decided it would be best for her to spend her limited free time with her family because she doesn't have much of it," she started crying uncontrollably.

The two of them broke down in tears as Ocean went to embrace her. "Oh no, that's awful news!"

After they had both settled down, Ocean remarked, "I noticed the grief in your eyes, let's stay in the time and make memories, your mother is still with us and let's cherish the moment, who knows what's going to come next."

It surprised Olivia that these statements were being spoken by someone who sounded like Ocean.

Ocean repeated herself to alter the topic. "I'll phone Collin to find out where he is and tell him to come over for supper," she said.

She attempted to call Collin twice, but each time his cell phone was turned off. She was positive he had gone in search of Della.

Collin entered the room as the hall gate suddenly opened. He had unkempt hair and no longer appeared to have any dressings on his head, and he appeared worried and fearful.

When Mr. Criss stepped forward to assist him, he was shoved aside and yelled, "This is all your fault, you sent Della off, what have you caused to that unfortunate girl?"

He then began to weep like a small girl, so Ocean and Olivia hurried to comfort him so that Ava wouldn't be disturbed.

Ocean requested Olivia's permission to look after him, then after she went in front of him and held his hands for the very first time, she led the way to his bedroom.

She stepped over and grasped his frozen hand; he wasn't even asking where Ocean was taking him; she wanted to take him to his own room, but he preferred to go to his suite.

"I wish I could help you or take away some of your suffering since I know how painful it is to love someone and have them neglect you," Ocean said as she sat near him and on the chair.

"What do you know about love," Collin questioned, turning to face her. "Do you know that I searched for her all day today despite being told she had left the country and changed her address? I tried calling her phone numerous times, but each time it went dead. She ran away with someone else and left me alone."

Although it wasn't the appropriate time, Ocean wanted she could tell him everything.

Collin was instructed to change, but instead of doing so, he got up and started destroying Della's photographs.

"She never wanted me, how much I attempted to fight for her with my family, mostly because of her my mother nearly died, but yet I stand behind her and she ran away with another guy. What he offered her which I couldn't provide?"

He was yelling and destroying the decorations by throwing things away.

Ocean was merely standing by, letting him vent his rage, or perhaps she was even enjoying seeing him wreck the room that he had built for Della!

He eventually became calmer, began to cry, and felt guilty for what he had done. "Oh my God, look at what I did! What if Della came back and wanted to live with me in this house someday? I tore her room apart! What I want to tell her?" inquiring while observing Ocean!

After wiping his face and helping him stand up from the floor, Ocean gave him his clothing and said, "Go ahead."

"I will wait here for you?"

Ocean helped him get ready and then led him to bed. When she was ready to leave, Collin grabbed her hand and asked, "Who are you? Why do you want to assist me? Why do I feel so connected to you?"

"I am similar as you, a girl who is broken in her love, who is striving to prove her affections to him but he is in love with someone else," Ocean said as she returned and sat next to him in bed. "I am your nurse, and I have decided to stay by your side until you are no longer in need of me."

Collin wouldn't let go of her hand. He was looking directly into her eyes. Although he was tempted to ask her to stay in his room, he decided against it.

Ocean was grinning as she walked away, delighted that Collin had stroked her hands, and surprised that it would be so challenging to share a little romance with the person she loved.

Perhaps all they needed was a little bit of affection, so she wished she could stay in bed with him, keeping him in her arm as he dozed off.

Outside the room, Olivia and Criss were waiting.

"We considered staying outside and letting you take care of things instead," Olivia commented.

"You did the right thing," she remarked.

"He needed to release the stress, and I let him. Soon, he became exhausted and wanted to sleep. I was glad he could rest," Ocean replied happily!

Chapter Fourteen
My Love Is Pure

Ocean made sure to get up early the following morning and clean up the messes Collin left behind the previous evening. She was making an effort to work softly so as not to wake him up.

While working, she paused and turned to look at Collin as, even though he was asleep, he still managed to capture her attention.

She arrived downstairs when the cleaning was done and saw that everyone in the family was seated at the breakfast table. She was glad to see Ava, who looked extremely under the weather and whose hands were shaking while attempting to grip the spoon.

She moved a chair across and sat down at the table after wishing everyone a good morning. Ava was searching the area to see if she could locate Collin.

"He was asleep, so there's no need to worry; when he wakes up, I'm sure he'll come downstairs," Ocean remarked.

Ocean noticed that Criss and Olivia were looking dejected and that it must have been difficult for them to pretend, she was the one who spoke again. "I hid Collin's mother's existence from him last night because I wanted him to be amazed when he saw her here."

"I am intending to invite your parents today, after all, they must have missed you," Ava remarked with a smile.

"Oh, Ava, that is the smartest idea; I don't understand why I never came up with this concept earlier."

"You had never given anything sufficient thought," Ava remarked as she averted her face away from him. Otherwise, our lives would be simpler."

Mr. Criss lowered his head down and just tried to occupy himself with the meal.

Ocean glanced at Olivia and nodded for her to speak up and get involved, but before Olivia could begin, Collin came down the stairs looking sharply dressed, clean-shaven, and prepared for the day.

When he saw Collin, Criss quickly got up from the table so they wouldn't get into a fight.

"You have no idea how overjoyed I am to see you here, Mom. It was my intention to come to see you in the hospital today, oh my gosh, I am so excited you are back." Collin rushed and hugged her and began kissing her face.

Ocean swiftly got up to leave the table when he pulled out a chair because it was awkward for a caretaker to eat at the same table as their boss.

"Where are you heading, my dear? Please sit down next to Collin; I want to see you two around each other," Ava halted her, asking.

Although Olivia was aware that she was the one who needed to inform her mother about Collin and Ocean's relationship at home, she was overlooked.

"Mom, don't worry, Ms. Ocean is just getting Collin's prescriptions ready for him. She's a nurse, after all, and only she would know what he needs to take every morning."

Ava appeared astonished, but Olivia tried to wink at her so she wouldn't say anything else.

"After everything you did for me last night, Ms. Ocean, please join us for breakfast. This is the least way I can express my gratitude to you."

Everyone was quiet, it was a slightly awkward scenario, and Ocean was acting as a caregiver in front of Collin's family while also appearing frightened.

Before any additional secrets could be revealed, she said, "I didn't do anything. I simply performed my job, thank you for your compassion." Then she walked away from the table.

"It is clear that she still feels awkward among us, but don't worry, mum, she will eventually grow used to this family."

In response to Olivia's comment as she saw Ocean go, Collin had a lengthy conversation with his mother and sister over breakfast, making him pleased. Mr. Criss had no impact on their happiness because he knew that as soon as either of them spotted him, their attitude would change.

After some while, Collin departed, but he wasn't sure if he needed to go to work or continue looking for Della. He was sitting in his car when he decided to try his luck once more. He began searching wherever he had been with Della, as well as calling their mutual friends to inquire concerning her whereabouts.

Soon, he began to grow weary and wondered if Della's money would run out whether or not she would return to him and request more. His head began to hurt severely as he abruptly became irritated with himself. He made the decision to go to work and spend some time there in the hopes that he would be so busy that he would forget about Della and that he'd also miss his friend Darsh.

***

Ocean was delighted to have her parents join them for supper that evening.

Ava was doing her best to be chatty and show Ocean's family that Ocean is in safe hands as they arrived early with some of Ocean's garments and books for her.

Ocean wished she had an answer for Raya's inquiry about her return date, but she made an effort to ignore it as she continued to give her hugs and asking when she would be returning.

While asking the housekeeper to bring them a drink, Aiden and Criss got busy playing chess together in the hall's corner like they used to.

Everything had returned to normal, and everyone was attempting to seem as though nothing had happened while bringing up various subjects of conversation.

Collin and Darsh arrived at the same time, and Olivia was so happy to see her love there that she started blushing.

Ocean was the only one who was familiar with their tale, and the others were unaware of Olivia's affections for Darsh.

Ocean stressed that her family should only be referred to as visitors and not introduced to Collin as who they are.

Collin greeted the Ocean family before entering his room. Ocean attempted to occupy herself by reading the magazine while Darsh and Olivia also vanished and headed to the garden, but her thoughts were on Collin and she was wondering about his day.

She made the decision to enter Collin's room upstairs without anyone noticing. Ocean overheard him conversing with a person as he was leaving voicemails for Della. "I know I don't deserve your love, but please understand that I'm trying my best. I can't live without you. It is difficult to persuade this family."

Ocean dragged a chair outside and sat behind the door, unsure of Collin's prognosis or whether his memory would ever return. She began to feel sorry for herself once more as the door suddenly opened and he noticed her.

"Why are you listening to my conversation with my wife, don't you have someplace better to be, besides spying on me?"

Ocean got to her feet. "I came to see if you needed anything, but I overheard you conversing, hence I decided to wait outside so as not to disturb you. I'm sorry."

Collin asked her to enter while keeping the door open and removing his jacket and tie. As soon as Ocean entered the room, he swiftly shut the door and remarked, "I don't know why, but my father doesn't like me at all. He's my strongest enemy in life. I assumed he asked you to follow me. By the way, I've never seen those people downstairs. Who are they? In this house, strange things are happening all the time that I am completely unaware of."

He was trying to take off his clothing while also chatting to Ocean, who was still standing. Ocean wanted to beg him to let her out of the room so he could change, but he kept talking instead.

In the meantime, Darsh and Olivia knocked on the door and entered the room without Collin's permission. Upon finding Colling standing with his briefs on and Ocean carrying his garments, they both started to giggle and hurriedly left the room, apologizing for disturbing them.

Darsh yelled out while he was still laughing, "Collin, brother, please keep the door locked next time."

Ocean was keeping her eyes closed the majority of the time, but she didn't mind either. It was embarrassing, of course, and that was the moment Collin understood what he was doing.

Ocean left the clothing on his bed while Collin hurriedly ran into the restroom.

She retreated to the corner where no one could see her and cleared her head because she couldn't stop giggling.

She was overcome with adult emotions, and she was incredibly grateful to have shared that moment with Collin.

After a short while, Collin was prepared, and he went downstairs to eat supper with the family and the visitor.

"Dear, was your mission successful, or not?" While they were serving dinner, Darsh was asking him questions, and somehow Ocean overheard them as well.

"I was chatting and therefore cut up in the moment that I totally forgot what I was doing, so shut up, nothing happened."

Ocean didn't want to look at him since she was uncomfortable, so she just winked at him as she passed by.

Whatever it was, Collin liked what he was experiencing about this lady. He was confident in her ability to be trusted.

Ocean resolved to remain up that night and document every single event that took place. She was aware that these were extremely uncommon occurrences, making any girl laugh just thinking about them.

Chapter Fifteen
Right to My Heart

The following day, everything appeared to be fine or perhaps different, and Ocean felt more at ease staying after what had transpired between them the previous day. She believed that this could be the beginning of a closer relationship with Collin.

Ava and Olivia were busy deciding on a night out and setting their jewelry because Collin's family had been invited to a large party in the city.

While Ocean was in the kitchen discussing Collin's diet plan with the house keepers, Collin was still in his room.

"It's a special night where we can all have fun, dance, eat, and drink while being present in the moment," Olivia interjected. "Aren't you planning to wear anything for tonight?"

Ocean stepped out of the kitchen and joined Olivia. "I'd love to join, but only if Collin could accompany me. Without him, it wouldn't be as much fun."

Olivia was certain that Collin would reject any party or ceremony if he found out about it, so she said, "Collin is not particularly fun when it comes to having fun, so don't expect him to join us, but I can have a company, maybe we can both enjoy ourselves without any man, just girls' night!" Ocean was not pleased.

"Can I let you know once I speak with Collin?"

"Let's go and wake him up and ask him," Olivia murmured, pulling her hand.

Ocean refused to enter and insisted that Olivia wake up her brother while she stayed in her room when they walked upstairs.

"Knock, knock, lazy brother, do you know what time it is? It will soon be afternoon." She opened the door and entered when no one responded.

While Collin was in the shower, Olivia shouted, "Collin," to be sure he could hear her. "If you are finished, please come out quickly since I am waiting here for you."

After a little while, Collin emerged from the bathroom wearing only a towel, asking Olivia, who was seated on his bed, "May I know what is my little sister doing here? For sure it is something significant, which has caused you to come to me instead of waiting."

While he awaited Olivia, he was making an effort to dry his hair with the towel.

"The reception for Mr. Robinson is tonight; I hope you remember them! Please come with us since we are all preparing to go."

"Look another way, I want to dress," he said.

"You are quite aware of the fact that I dislike gatherings where I am always being watched and where everyone wants to make me dance with their daughters."

Olivia just had a thought. "What if you asked Ocean to be your companion tonight? That way, nobody would bother you, and we would all get what we wanted."

"Ocean will never accept to be with me," Collin remarked after pausing for a while to consider her proposal. "She has a lover, and I'm sure she won't be comfortable."

Olivia grinned at him and said, "I'm sure she'll agree if you insist. She also needs to leave this place, so this is a fantastic opportunity for all of us."

"Ocean is in her room, so act like a gentleman and go ask her respectfully if she would like to go to the salon for her hair and makeup after lunch. If she does, please let me know so I may bring her along."

"Why do you believe she needs to visit a salon, Olivia? She doesn't even need to wear makeup or a fancy outfit to be attractive."

When Olivia turned to face Collin, she was overjoyed to find that her brother had made such a kind remark about Ocean.

Collin was shocked by his own words as well because he had no idea how deeply Ocean had affected him.

He waited until Olivia had left, and once he was by himself, he began to question if he really wanted to invite Ocean to the night party.

The door was open when he arrived at Ocean's room, and he noticed her writing something there. He knocked on the door, and Ocean allowed him in, without turning around to see who it was.

"I'm here to ask you a question, Ms. Ocean."

Ocean leapt up from her chair and swiftly turned around, believing Olivia had come to tell her about the talk she had with Collin. Collin's being there greatly startled her.

"I apologize if I disturbed you. I did knock, before entering!"

Ocean struggled to keep her feelings in check and replied with a smile, "I was just writing in my journal, I'm writing all this so I can share everything with my partner. You didn't bother me!"

After Della, Collin had not asked any other girls out because he was a little terrified of being turned down.

He therefore sat in the corner chair. He had to express what he had come for when he realized Ocean was genuinely lovely and said, "I came here to invite you to be my date tonight? Please don't take offense if I called you a date; I was simply trying to find out if you would like to join me and my family."

Ocean's jaw gaped in shock as she realized Collin had offered to her. "It will be good once in a while to meet new people," she responded while attempting to keep her hair out of her face with one hand.

"So, I take it to be yes?"

While he was staring at her so intently, Collin questioned her once more. Ocean grinned and replied, "Yes."

Ocean was so thrilled when Collin left the room that she couldn't even describe it. Instead, she simply wrote in her notebook, "My love asked me for a night out, this is our first time going to any dance party."

Unfortunately, she had not packed any party dresses, so she had to make do with just one sky blue, silky, long dress that had no sleeves. She believed that although it wasn't particularly fancy, it was still better than the outfit she had been wearing in front of Collin every day.

Ocean spoke to her mother on the phone and detailed everything that had occurred. "Just be yourself tonight and avoid being like the nurse, I'm sure you two will love it," Raya advised her.

Ava, with the assistance of Olivia, headed for the hairdresser since she wanted her mother to think differently and joyful.

Ocean made the decision to stay and travel with Collin. She was happy and anxious at the same time. Her mother had advised her to be herself, but how could she do that?

What would Collin be thinking of her? She was unsure of how she should behave.

Since Mr. Criss was the only lonely person at home, Ocean went to his room and inquired, "Are you sure you want to stay, Mr. Criss?"

When Criss noticed Ocean there while he was busy reading the news, he set the papers aside and invited Ocean to come join him, saying, "Come on in, my dear Ocean."

"I'm not sure if you being alone here is a good idea, this family needs you as well," said Ocean as she entered and sat down next to the gentleman.

"I know that and, I need them too, but my heart is so sad, I feel terrible," cried Criss as he sobbed. "I can't just stare at Ava's face since I know she will soon pass away, which makes me feel even worse. On the other hand, I wished Collin had forgotten all of his memories, including the fact that I am his father. When I look at him, I feel embarrassed of myself."

"We all make errors; we can't help it, but the gates of compassion are always accessible," replied Ocean as he handed him a handkerchief. "Ava is still living and needs a partner, and Collin has escaped the tragedy and is standing by your side in good health, so there is still time to set things right. You now have one final opportunity to put things correct."

"These things coming out of your mouth at this age make me believe that Aiden has really raised a lovely, strong woman," stated Criss, shaking his head as he gave her a loving gaze.

Then he got to his feet and said, "You're right, my sweetie. I'll go get ready, so we can go together."

Also, Ocean got to his feet and added, "I'll be coming with Collin. He invited me to join him tonight. I hope it's alright with you? However, after an hour, you may pick up the other two lovely beauties from the salon!"

Ocean received a kiss on the forehead from Criss, who then swiftly left to get ready after wishing her the best of luck for the evening.

Ocean clasped her hands and exclaimed how delighted she was to have made someone smile. When she got upstairs, she noticed that Collin's room had music playing, which was a signal of good things to come. She headed off to get ready.

She was soon ready, but she wasn't sure if she would actually look acceptable in front of Collin. Her hair was simple—she just brushed it and kept it open— and she didn't think much more could be done with it than a little mascara and red lipstick.

When she heard a knock at the door, her heartbeat quickened, so she requested Collin to enter. He was dressed in a cream-colored suit with a white shirt underneath and brown shoes. His shirt's bottoms were slightly open, and hair gel had been used to stylishly style his hair. Moreover, his fragrance was mesmerizing.

Ocean was on the verge of passing out when she saw her fiancé in that position, but Collin was more astonished than Ocean.

He was enraged to see Ocean in that silk dress as well as her hair and makeup since she had been wearing only jeans, a different T-shirt so often, and also no makeup.

Being unable to speak, Ocean grinned and inquired, "Am I that horrible that you can't comment on my appearance?"

When Collin realized he had been quiet for a little longer than usual, he calmed himself, reclaimed his voice, and said, "Oh my Gosh, I was not sure if it was actually you, I knew you are lovely, but I never imagined this!

"Can we go now?" he added as he excused himself.

Ocean answered, "Yes, please," while attempting to hide his strong reaction.

Collin was attempting to start a conversation in the car, but he was hesitant how.

"Do you let your boyfriend know you're going out with me?"

"He is in love with someone else, and it doesn't matter to him really," Ocean replied with a smile as she addressed him.

"Why would you choose to live in my house and cope with a cranky person like me? I'm sorry if I'm bothering you with these kinds of inquiries, but I didn't want to make you feel awkward. Your family appears to be wealthy, and you are both intelligent and attractive."

Ocean wished she could tell him everything, but she had to follow orders, and she couldn't tell him the truth until he had to recall them.

She turned to Collin and said, "My fiancé came after me because his family wanted him to, and he didn't tell me he was in love with someone else, and once I learned that he was in love with someone else, I made the decision to leave the house for a bit. I planned to travel to Spain.

"However, your father told my father about your accident, and I promised to assist. This was the ideal chance for me to go and occupy myself. This is how I came to be with you, then.

"In addition, I'm helping a lady pay off her house loan with the cash you're paying me. I wanted to keep this work so I could support her, so please don't tell anyone and I hope you've received your answers."

Then he turned to face Ocean and unintentionally crossed his hands with hers. He instantly corrected himself and said, "So we are almost both experiencing this pain!"

Everyone was expecting them as a couple and welcoming them as they almost arrived at the celebration. The nicest area, in Collin's opinion, was the one with the most mouthwatering desserts. There was a large hall with lovely arrangements, a live band on one side, a big bar at the other half, and nearly all of the young couples were seated there.

Ocean set out to find Olivia, and after some time, she discovered her dancing on stage with Darsh. With Mr. Robinson and his wife, Collin's parents were occupied in conversation.

Eventually, a table became available and Collin invited Ocean to sit at it while he placed an order for some drinks.

Soon when he returned, he offered Ocean one but she declined, saying, "I like to stay awake, one of us should drive back home."

After drinking his first glass, Collin turned to her and stated, "I appreciate the way you think."

Ocean was unsure of what he was doing because she knew Collin wasn't supposed to drink while on medication, but she didn't know how to stop him. Then he swiftly completed the second.

"Have you ever danced on a stage?" she enquired.

"I don't like to dance, but I like to observe. My girlfriend used to dance on stage with other guys, and she used to tell me my body is really tense. I was not a perfect fit." Then, all of a sudden, he grew silent and his formerly smiling face turned sour. He then got up from the table and left without offering an explanation.

Ocean was so surprised that she couldn't believe she had brought his bitter memories back to him. All she had wanted to do was get him to stop drinking, but out of the blue, she began to recall all the unpleasant experiences.

She was frightened and unsure of how to find her fiancé among all of those people. Once Olivia and Darsh arrived, they questioned Ocean why she had been sitting alone. When she described what had happened, they both were concerned.

Darsh concluded by saying, "I suppose I know where I can find him."

Since Collin enjoyed smoking after having a few shots of alcohol, Darsh went to a large balcony that was designated for smokers and found Collin there.

"I knew you were here, so why are you sitting by yourself when you could have invited me to join you?"

Collin's expression changed as if he had discovered something. "I can't love her the same way I used to. I know she's back, but with everything that has transpired between us, my love has changed. I used to wait for her to come back, but now I don't even like having her in my arm."

"Just go dance with her and you will forget it all, don't be so hard on yourself," Darsh said after he realized he was a little disoriented and didn't understand what Collin was saying.

"She left me, changed her address, and returned to this location to tell me what? She has come here, I'm sure, because her money is gone!"

Darsh began to realize that he had been mistaking Ocean for Della all this time!

What a terrible mistake Collin was making at the time!

"I have to ask her everything; I need to know why she had to leave and why she returned, as well as what our relationship is since I'm sick of it."

"Please don't tell her anything here, you can take her in the parking lot and ask her anything," Darsh said as he followed him out.

Collin shook his head in agreement with Darsh since he was practically drunken and couldn't think clearly.

Olivia and Ocean were taken aback to see Darsh and Collin arrive to the table instantly in such a rush.

When Collin saw his mother, he told the others, "No one will leave this table until I am back," and pointed to Ocean, saying, "specially you," before heading to where Ava was sitting in her wheelchair on the other side of the hallway.

Ocean and Olivia turned to face Darsh, who stated, "I think all the vodka and smokes have ruined his brain. He thinks Ocean is Della and wants to somehow take her downstairs in the parking lot to talk to her. I think Ocean you have to leave immediately."

"Why do you believe she has to leave?" Olivia said worriedly. "Collin needs her, so we all need to leave and accompany him. We also need to handle the matter carefully."

Ocean was at a loss for words and extremely upset. She had been hoping to dance on stage with Collin and spend a beautiful evening next to him. She didn't want to even speak as her tears were slowly streaming from her eyes.

"It was all my fault," Olivia continued, "I completely forgot Collin was not permitted to use any drink and also compelled you to come with him. I'll get him fixed, so don't worry. Every one of us must depart at once."

Ocean was just being quiet. She found it annoying that she thought Collin was beginning to like her, especially when he had previously betrayed her and been with Della. She reasoned that she could start over with him. Collin was still ailing, though.

When Collin got back, he was still in a foul mood. "Della, follow me to the car, and the rest of you don't mention anything to Mom and Dad that you have seen Della in this party, or else I have to answer hundreds of questions later to both of them," he said.

"Don't worry, I can handle him—he's still Collin," Ocean said as he stood up and walked away from them. "And, don't tell Mrs. Ava what's going on; she's simply having a good time with Mr. Criss." Ocean wiped away her tears and left.

"Maybe we should just let them get along; it could be best to let her manage things. She wants to spend the rest of her life with Collin; let her see what and how he can be. She can then decide later on whether or not she actually wants to continue." They both concurred after Darsh made a comment.

"May I please drive?" before stepping into the automobile, Ocean questioned.

"Where did you leave your own vehicle?" Collin inquired.

"I came in a taxi, is it at the garage?"

Then he handed her the keys, and while she was driving, Collin was the one talking to her about her absence, her travels, and other things. Ocean broke down in tears despite her best efforts to contain them!

She came to the corner and stopped the car. "I am sorry, I am facing some problems and I had to informed you, my mistake, now I am back and I want to stay, please allow me."

Collin grasped her hand and kissed it. Ocean had just remembered how his hand had accidentally crossed hers as they were heading to the party, so he swiftly removed it. Now, he was continuing to kiss her hand without stopping. He then moved closer to kiss her eyes and lips, but she prevented him.

"Should we go to your house? I have a lot I'd want to tell you," Ocean stated.

Collin, who had before been chatty, had now become obedient and quiet. He spent the entire time holding Ocean's hand on his chest while keeping his eyes closed.

Ocean knew the route and took Collin to his room as soon as they arrived at his house.

"My love, come, let me show you our chamber. Starting tonight, we'll stay in this space and nothing will be able to keep us apart."

Ocean turned to face the room as Collin began to describe all the decorations and designs, as well as the lengths he went to in order to arrange them for her.

Ocean told Collin to get ready in bed while she used the restroom to pamper herself and then come to bed, but not before giving Collin two tablets.

Collin was ecstatic and changed into pajamas before going to bed, but he struggled to stay up for very long because of the sleeping medications he had taken.

Ocean was hiding in the toilet when she noticed Collin dozing off quickly. She stepped out, covered him in a kiss, and then she went.

She went to her room, sobbed for her misfortune, and then called her mother to tell her that everything had gone as planned and that she had returned home. She didn't want to worry her parents because, in the end, it was her decision.

Chapter Sixteen
Find Your Way Back

The following morning, Ocean was so exhausted and drained that she didn't want to leave her bed. She was unsure of how to proceed and whether what she was doing would ever have an impact on Collin and restore him to his former self.

She was considering both scenarios. Collin still recalls Della; she was Della before the accident and she always will be the same. Sadly, she'll never get the chance to be loved and seen.

There were times when she wished Collin would never revert to his old self so they could begin a new relationship.

She sobbed and hid behind her blanket because she was heartbroken and devastated.

One of the housemaids eventually called her name and requested permission to enter after a short while.

Ocean wiped her tears quickly. "Please enter, my dear."

"Mam, something awful has occurred. I went to Madam Eva's chamber to give her medicine, but she didn't open her eyes, her hands were cold, and I don't think she has a heartbeat.

"As you are the only person in this house who can help, I came straight to you since I had no idea where to go or what to do."

Ocean didn't know how to get out of bed and had no time to dress or wash her face. She ran downstairs to Eva's room and saw that Eva had left by the look on her face.

While holding Eva's hand and comforting her as she sobbed, she called an ambulance and stated, "I'm sorry."

When Olivia saw her mother in that state and entered the room after being awakened by the noises, she began to sob and scream. Collin and Mr. Criss were also awakened.

That was the part that no one wants to think back on. When Olivia was yelling and sobbing in another corner, Mr. Criss was crying in one corner and the housekeeper was attempting to comfort him.

While holding his mother in his arms and attempting to keep her hair out of her face, Collin remained silent and helplessly holding out no words. After kissing her forehead, he covered her with a sheet.

Although nobody was making eye contact with him, Ocean was watching him. When the paramedics arrived, it was tragically confirmed that she had passed away.

When Collin stood there and saw what they were doing, Ocean approached, grabbed his hand and led the way to his room.

When she was about to leave after giving him his prescription and putting him back to bed, he grabbed her hand and asked, "Please, Ms. Ocean, remain a while with me in the bed."

When Ocean realized he recognized her, she didn't mind sharing a bed with him. He then held Ocean's hand before quickly falling asleep again.

Ocean told her parents what had happened and asked them for aid; shortly, other members of her family and friends were also notified.

Ocean was glad that both Mr. Mason (Darsh's father) and Darsh were present to help. The funeral was the next day, but Mr. Criss was unsure about Collin's capacity to handle everything.

***

Everyone was prepared for the funeral; however, Ocean had to stay at home with Collin since he was in bed and the doctors were attempting to keep him quiet there because they believed he was in shock and should avoid being involved in any formalities or interactions with other people.

"I believe you need to spend a few days at home with us; this atmosphere is not healthy for you. Look at your situation, you seem so worn. You have been trying to take care of everyone, but who will take care of you?" Raya exclaimed once they arrived at Mr. Criss' home.

Ocean tried not to talk about herself in front of other people since she was extremely exhausted and her mother was right because strange things kept happening in that family.

"Do you recall what I said a year ago when you and your father were preparing to leave Madrid and travel back to your native country? I begged you both to let me stay longer and will join you when I believe the timing is right. Yet, you two maintained that since I had been gone for so long, it was the time for me to visit my parents' homeland."

Ocean sat on the corner chair with her parents joining her, saying, "Now I'm engaged even if I don't want to! And I am unable to pack up everything and escape. Look at Collin, her sister, and her father. Do you believe I can simply collect my bags and say farewell. Do not come after me and demand that I go back since the day you all brought me to this land was the day my life ended."

While sobbing, she got to her feet and up the stairs to go check on Collin.

She went to Collin's room after everyone else had left and discovered him staring out the window. "Do you prefer to stay at home or join them?"

Collin wasn't responding, as if his body and spirit were absent and he were in another universe.

Only one or two words were spoken by him. Ocean believed that as Collin's official nurse, her only responsibility was to ensure his safety.

To see if he could eat food, she led him to the table while holding his hand. As if he had just woken up, Collin appeared to be staring at her. "How are you so resilient in light of everything that has occurred in this home and in your life?"

Ocean didn't expect him to say something like that so she made a small attempt to style her hair and wiped her face with a tissue before declaring, "I need to be strong; otherwise, how can I do my job?"

"Yeah, I forgot, you are a nurse and seeing this kind of thing is so commonplace and evident for you people, you have become accustomed to them." He then took a piece of bread and put it in his mouth.

Then he was staring at Ocean's face and waiting for her to reply, Ocean was not ready for any kind of argument, she was not even sure if Collin was aware of the time and place he was in.

"Can I call you Ocean?" he asked.

Ocean shook her head and said, "Of course."

When he couldn't find his cigars in his drawers, he became angry and started throwing things while shouting at Ocean that he needed to smoke right away.

Ocean went and pulled the entire box out of the bathroom cupboard, lit one of them, and gave it to him.

When he took the cigarette from Ocean, his hand was trembling; she drew the chair for him and kept the window open so that fresh air might enter.

While smoking his cigar and sobbing, Collin said, "I met my mother's physician the day I went to the hospital for a test. He informed me about my mother and why he had to release her. That day, even though she was still alive, I stayed in the hospital and grieved for her, hoping I could pass away in her place. I wanted her to be content, so when I got home, I played I knew nothing."

He was unable to continue smoking, so Ocean quickly grabbed the cigar from his grasp and he continued saying, "If that night Della had not been shown up, my mother might still be alive; she hated Della and her heart condition couldn't take any more anxiety." Ocean also broke down in tears; she had never believed Collin was aware of his mother's condition.

She offered him a drink of water and asked him if he would like to go to the garden with her. "Ocean, my mother adored you. The night at the party, she told me Ocean is a decent lady. Try to grab her heart. You truly meant a lot to her."

Ocean wasn't sure if she should be thrilled to hear that or if she should grieve!

"Your mother was a sweet and compassionate lady. The previous few months, she had struggled greatly to continue alive, and she was a worrier, but her heart didn't allow her to continue. I wish she can rest at peace."

Collin was still not content and was filled with rage. "Della destroyed my family, she was the one who turned up from nowhere," he said. "I tried to take her away from that party shortly so no one will realize she has been there, but it looked my mother had already noticed her."

Ocean persuaded Collin to join her in the garden so they could work on some gardening since she had to act else, she knew he wouldn't stop talking about Della.

While Collin wasn't feeling well at the moment, he didn't mind because Ocean thought of no other way to cheer him up.

She urged him to engage in some gardening, planting, moving pots about, and attempting watering the plants. At first, Collin was confused, but later he also began aiding Ocean and found it enjoyable.

After an hour, he was exhausted and eager to get into bed. Recently, sleeping was the only activity that brought him comfort. Ocean suspected this might be a sign of sadness or a side effect of his medications.

One week went by in much the same way, with Ocean being nearly the only person connected to Collin. She was the nurse, and Collin was her dashing patient.

She was missing her family and her room, but she was unable to give up because Collin was so dependent on her these days and being left alone could have further harmed his soul.

Mr. Criss had already returned to work, rarely spent any time at home, and didn't even show up for a meal.

Olivia, whose primary occupation was painting, was constantly in her workshop and seemed to be working. Darsh frequently paid a visit to her and Collin as well.

Ocean's only companions these days were her journal and the garden. Even though her parents were there for brief visits nearly every day, she continued to feel alone and that she had lost herself in the process of adapting to the new circumstances.

When Ocean and her mother had plans to go shopping one day, Collin was already being taken care of by the housemaids who had been told what to do.

Ocean had a planned mother-daughter shopping trip one day. When she was dressed, she noticed Collin was waiting outside her room, dressed and prepared. "Ocean, I want to take you out tonight. Please come with me instead of going shopping with your mum."

Ocean was perplexed as to why Collin was inviting her out. She instantly recalled the last time he had, when he had confused her with Della, and she was unsure as to whether she should accept his invitation once more.

Yet she reasoned that there was nothing to lose by trying it again.

She quickly made a call to her mother, told her to postpone her shopping, and then she joined Collin.

She wanted to drive, but he insisted on taking the wheel. They quickly arrived at the old town theater, where it appeared that only one show has been running there for the past six years.

"They planned to tear it down and build some useless apartments, but I bought it and promised the actors and performers that as long as I am alive, this performance must be played for everyone and it should be free. This is my favorite site in the whole town.

"At the moment, they have more than 100 audience members per day, and don't worry, I pay the salaries of all the theater staff members."

Ocean found it hard to understand that her gruff fiancé had such a sweet heart and was so passionate about things that she hardly felt he could be a part of.

She was observing the theater the entire time from the entryway, where there were pictures of actors and actresses from the 1970s and 1980s. The structure was incredibly well-maintained despite its age; inside, it was like a museum.

"I am in awe; I had no idea you were a fan of arts, particularly these types."

"There are a lot of things about me you don't know, and we have only just begun," Collin added as he drew nearer to her and grabbed her hand.

Ocean could feel Collin's hand warming up to her and the way he was holding it, like if he never wanted to let go.

She wished there was a way to capture this beautiful feeling in time.

At the first floor VIP area, Collin had special seating arranged for him. Collin sat next to Ocean after helping her take her seat. Before the performance, a variety of refreshments were served.

Ocean forgot about Collin, who had been focused solely on her and her reactions, after the concert had begun since she had become totally engrossed in the narrative. He appeared to know her for a very long time by the way he was staring at her.

The storyline of the program concerned a boy who lost his sight while serving in the military and struggled to locate his wife and children when he got home.

Ocean was in tears after the show and only then did she realize that Collin had been holding her hand the entire time.

"Did you enjoy it?" he said as he handed her a tissue.

"When I turned ten, I went to theater for the last time; after that, I never tried to go. I'm so happy I decided against shopping."

The two of them then began to giggle, and ultimately, they departed the area.

They approached a small van that was parked next to the park on their way back, and Collin said to Ocean, "I hope you are hungry because you are going to eat the world's testiest burger."

She said, "I can't wait," despite the fact that she was already full.

After placing the meal order, he went to the car and urged Ocean to come sit outside. Ocean complied with his instructions. She found it hard to comprehend that all of that beauty could fit within one frame. The twilight, the stream, the flowers, and the woods!

"Did I do anything wrong that has caused you to cry?" Collin questioned as tears were streaming from her eyes.

"Everything in my life is moving at such a rapid pace that I wish I had the ability to freeze these moments," Ocean stated after wiping away her tears and saying, "I have missed all these."

These moments haven't only come into your life for a short while, Collin assured her, "These moments have come to stay because you earned them." Collin then grasped her hand.

When their food eventually arrived, they both ate eagerly. Ocean couldn't believe she was eating the sloppy burger in front of Collin since her outfits was covered in ketchup.

They returned home after eating. "I wanted to express my gratitude to you and let you know how grateful I am that you chose to be my nurse. I also wished you a good evening's rest. I was at a loss as to how to convey my respect, so I reasoned that a night out could be beneficial."

"I'm so happy to finally meet the genuine Collin. You don't have to say thank you all the time, however please know that I appreciated every moment of tonight."

"What could I call this night, how else could I explain it, whatever that was, I pray I could do it again, and thank God for this living," In her diary, Ocean had written these final words just before going to sleep.

Chapter Seventeen
The Last Time

Ocean awoke rather late, had a restful night's sleep, and wondered if everything that transpired the previous evening was just a story. She wasn't sure if Collin still remembered what had taken place that evening.

She quickly got out of bed, changed, and went to check on Collin. Surprisingly, he wasn't there. Since his mother had died, he had been staying at home and hadn't seen the need to go out much. But on this particular day, he had left a note for Ocean saying, "I will come back for dinner, don't stress about me, I had a good night's sleep and I am perfectly alright."

Ocean inhaled deeply and decided that today would be a good day to take a break and spend more time with Olivia, Oliva was still in her nightgown when she entered her room, but she didn't look well at all.

"Good morning, Olivia. How are you doing? Do you believe Collin went to work today?"

"I am glad for him," she said, not really in the mood for chat.

"Are you all right? Do you need to talk?"

She brushed away her tears and said, "I'm lost, I thought I would get over Darsh but I couldn't. He's getting engaged next Saturday and I have to stand and witness all that."

Ocean became quite concerned and said, "I thought you both had agreed not to be married and to remain single so that you could be with each other."

"Indeed, this was a plan, but my uncle has pushed that Darsh get married as soon as possible since they feel that this family needs some joy and good news," Olivia began sobbing more vehemently.

"Wishing there was a way to inform Collin of everything," Ocean remarked as she moved her chair toward Olivia's seat.

"Collin knew everything and was prepared to assist, but after his injury he does not remember anything about my narrative with Darsh, therefore I don't believe it is a good idea to include him since his memory is still foggy!"

Ocean recognized her accuracy. She excused herself to go after hearing a phone ring in Collin's room and speculated that he might have called with a request.

"Who is this, hello?" But nobody responded. After cutting off the call, phone rang again, but this time there was no response as well.

Considering she was unable to hear anything on the phone, Ocean wondered whether there might be a problem with the connections.

She returned to her room and began wondering about Olivia and Darsh and what their future would hold.

***

Mr. Criss returned home in the afternoon. Before his wife passed away, he used to enquire about Ocean and engage in candid conversations about her relationship with Collin every day, but lately he had fallen into a state of silence.

Ocean had the idea to go see him because she was also quite lonely. He appeared to be in another world as he sat quietly holding the TV remote while the screen was still off.

"Good afternoon, Mr. Criss, hoping you are doing well today. Is it okay if I may sit with you for a little while?" she said as she moved forward so he could see her.

"My child, you don't need to be so official with me, I am just like your dad, please sit down with me," said Criss, who appeared to have just awakened.

He was about to smoke but stopped himself, saying, "Old habit, Ava constantly wanted me to stop smoking, since she felt this could kill me one day, but right now I am still living and inhaling and she is the one who has sadly died."

"It's so difficult to think that she is no longer with us. Well perhaps, she is now in a good place," Ocean remarked.

Criss nodded in agreement with what Ocean had just spoken, "I'm not here today for myself, I'm here to talk with you concerning Olivia. I hope you won't take it personally, and if you can, please try to help her."

Since this was the first time Ocean had spoken openly about anyone outside herself and Collin, he became a little concerned when he heard Olivia's name.

"What's going on with Olivia, my dear daughter? I know I've been neglecting her for a very long time, but please know that I'll do anything I can to help."

"Someone needs to act now before it's too late, but I'm not sure whether I should speak about it or not," she said. "Darsh and Olivia have always been in love, and they like one other and planned to get married.

"Darsh is getting engaged next week, and Olivia is going wild here," she said after pausing briefly to gauge Mr. Criss' emotion, after she had noticed he was interested in knowing more, she continued, "Collin was aware of their narrative as they both came to him for assistance, but since his injury, he has forgotten everything.

"I am entirely opposed to the traditional family weddings that are taking place in this part of the world and I do not support such, but as Olivia's friend, I am pleading with you to respect their right to live their lives as they choose. I don't want this family to have a tragic ending to everyone!"

He didn't appear startled at all and said, "To be completely honest, I have seen their affection for one another for a very long time, but I didn't want to say anything. I was expecting for one of them to reach out to me and tell me what was happening, but it seems that none of them were ready to discuss."

He inhaled deeply before saying, "I developed that rule to make other people's life simpler, I wanted everyone to know they are free to choose their partners from elsewhere as well. Indeed, my brother had spoken to me about his intentions for Darsh, but I was unaware that he would shortly become engaged."

After that, he got to his feet and searched for his cell phone. He then called his brother, asking him to come over and bring along Darsh. Ocean was a little anxious because she didn't know what would occur.

"Let's wait for them to arrive. I want both of them to acknowledge what the conditions are for their marriage and that they must concur with all of them. Family marriages are difficult because there are so many assumptions, however my brother and I have both gone through it, so we both understand what it's like."

Ocean decided that Olivia needed to know since she was worried that she would be annoyed with her for the rest of her life. She also got up, hugged Mr. Criss, and said, "Please make Olivia smile; she has lost a mom!"

He gave me Ocean a hug in return and promised to do that, so she excused myself and went to Olivia's room. She was dozing on her bed with a blanket over her, so Ocean called her name to see if she was awake.

"Olivia, sweetheart, are you a wake? I have exciting news for you!"

Suddenly she poked her head out from the blanket and exclaimed, "The only good news in my life is my end coming!"

Then Ocean leaped into her bed and fully undid the blanket covering her. She began by recounting her interaction with Mr. Criss and anything that had occurred just a few minutes before.

At first, Olivia was confused by what had just transpired. Then, her grief turned to excitement and she began shouting with joy. They both held hands and started bouncing on the mattresses as Olivia continued to kiss and hug Ocean endlessly.

Very quickly, Ocean assisted her in getting dressed and prepared for Darsh's arrival. She was unable to express her gratitude to Ocean, alternately crying and smiling.

"I want to ask that you don't fight with your dad, he has committed to assisting both of you, he has experienced the same thing while his life with his cousin who turned out to be your mother, so please pay attention to him wisely and think before you comply to anything," Ocean said to Olivia as she was designing her hair.

She hugged Ocean and said, "I'll guarantee you; I've waited my whole life for this moment, and I won't destroy it."

The bell rang as they left the room, and they both grinned as they gazed at one another.

"Collin has said he'll be back for supper." So, Ocean excused herself to go start cooking. In fact, she wanted to give the family very little privacy.

Ocean was concerned that she would suffer the consequences if things didn't turn out as she had hoped.

Following their arrival, Darsh and his father walked and sat down next to Mr. Criss in the hallway. Mr. Criss then summoned Olivia, who was already hiding in the kitchen.

After greeting them, he immediately began probing both of them with a few questions before saying, "My brother and I were both aware of your feelings for one another, but we didn't want to push anything. We were pressured by our parents to choose our bride from among the relatives, and sometimes that option was not even available, but we didn't want to go on with this tradition any longer because of the health problems that would cause in the future."

Darsh's father continued, "We both lost children and experienced health issues solely as a result of the fact that we were related. You have to agree to anything that both families want of you, and you can never obtain a separation if you're related. We don't mind, but if you agree, there may be ups and downs in the future due to your marriage."

Even if they had not yet considered all of this, Darsh and Olivia understood exactly what each other meant and still desired to be together.

Darsh stood up and declared, "Olivia is the love of my life. I have chosen her freely and without pressure, and I will guarantee her that no matter what happens, I will remain by her. Even if I have to give up on having a child, I will still return to her."

The two brothers then waited for Olivia to speak. She was hesitant to do so because she knew it was either now or never.

"I never could look at Darsh as my brother, because I knew the feelings inside me were different. Yes, I know many others around the globe utterly despise this, but I am not living my life to please people around me. I want to do what I want and this time I am saying it loud and clear, I will accept Darsh and I will understand all the difficulties this is going to cause us in the long term, since I know, when he is by my side, nothing would be impossible."

The two brothers then applauded them and thanked them for their decisions.

Ocean was crying the entire time she was upstairs listening to the conversation since she was so happy because of it.

Chapter Eighteen
Please Talk Back

After getting out of bed, Ocean reasoned that since nothing but good had occurred over the previous two days, this family's season may get off to a nice start.

As she waited for Collin last night until late, she was unsure if he was going to the office. But he had previously told Darsh that he would be somewhat busy there because the final person performing their digital marketing had left, and he had to handle that portion as well.

She felt sorry for Collin because he had to work so hard, and at occasions she wished to let him know that she could assist him at work as well, but she was content with their dating life and didn't want to end it.

Collin learned of Olivia's engagement, and he was thrilled to learn that two of his closest friends were getting married.

The phone rang while Ocean was getting ready for the day, and since she didn't hear anyone answering it, she knew Collin wasn't there. A short while later, the phone began to ring again, and this time Ocean hurried to Collin's room. When she didn't find him there, she swiftly picked up the phone.

"Hi, may I help you?"

It took a moment before the person on the other end of the telephone could be heard saying, "I don't know whether you really can, help me, but tell me first who are you and what you're doing in Collin's apartment?"

Ocean abruptly cut the line because she was startled by the woman's voice and felt threatened.

She hesitated for a moment before answering the phone when it rang again, and when she did, she said, "Why are you disconnecting the connection, do you know Collin is my lover, do you know who I am now?" without saying anything further.

Ocean was forced to respond. "You've wounded this family a lot, so you're not wanted here or anywhere else close to them. I think it's best if you just vanish into thin air and pretend you never existed."

"Such a big mouth for such a little character; I now know who you are; you were the one who pushed herself upon Collin. Not in this life or in Collin's prior life, you drove him to pursue you despite the fact that he fired you from your post. You never had a solid position and he will never want you. I'm back and I want my boyfriend. Watch me how it is will take him."

Ocean hung up the phone while her hand was shaking and she still couldn't imagine what had happened. As she stood up to leave the room, the phone started to ring again. This time, Collin, who had been in the shower the entire time, rushed out to try to answer it.

He said good morning to Ocean and immediately answered the phone. After a little moment, he broke down in tears and asked, "Am I dreaming? Della, is it really you? Where have you been? How on earth could you abandon me? Do you realize that my mother has passed away? If so, please come to me."

When he turned around and saw Ocean still standing there, he said, "Please leave the room; I need some privacy."

With all the sacrifices she had made, Ocean was in tears as she left the room, and even though he was pursuing Della, she was heartbroken.

Olivia, after setting the breakfast table and coming upstairs to check on them to see why they were both late to the meal, she retreated to Ocean's room who was sobbing loudly. Olivia was also felt afraid and anxious.

Ocean responded while lying down on her bed when she asked her what had gone wrong.

"She's back, she's in the city, but I thought you guys said she was gone for good," while yelling, she asked Olivia.

Olivia hurriedly shut the door and approached her, asking, "Are you referring to Della? How did you find out?"

"I picked up Collin's phone while he was in the shower, and she stated she had come to get him back; unfortunately, Collin was already on the phone with her."

When Collin eventually exited his room, he went straight to Ocean's and discovered Olivia there as well.

"Why did you answer my phone, Ms. Ocean? I told you to take care of your own affairs and not meddle with mine on the first day you joined. If you can abide by this guideline, feel free to stay; if not, please leave my home instantly."

After speaking with Della, Collin seemed like a different guy to Olivia. She requested that Collin recognize Ocean as a part of the family.

Collin apologized before leaving the room with an irritated expression on his face as if he could not hear anything.

Olivia felt terrible for Ocean because of everything she had done.

"I'm sorry, but I have to tell my father that she's returned; this is not at all good.

"She is wicked and has already exacted revenge on us, but she is still unsatisfied, and it appears that she won't stop until she has destroyed each of us."

After that, she hurried downstairs to tell her father. Ocean was frozen in bed because she wasn't sure whether staying any longer was appropriate given what Collin had said.

She began to collect her belongings since she didn't want Collin to continue to harm her feelings.

Ocean descended the stairs holding her handbag. Olivia stopped her in her tracks, and Mr. Criss joined them. He took the bags from Ocean and pleaded with her not to give up because she had gone so far and was so close to Collin. "I also needed Ocean's assistance, as did Collin and Olivia. Give me some time, I'll get everything fixed," he stated.

"I'm exhausted, I can't do this any longer, I have to end this," Ocean cried.

"I'll ask the driver to take you home. You need to spend some time with your folks. Maybe after you've been gone for a bit, you'll decide better. I know you're hurt and exhausted," Mr. Criss said.

Olivia didn't want to let her go since she was simply in the urge to celebrate her delight with everyone and didn't think she needed to stop as Della had been returned once more.

"Ocean, please don't mind Collin's foolishness; you know he is not himself and he doesn't realize what he's doing. I hope I had the ability to remind him of the past, but I am afraid of losing him forever. If he learns Della is our sister, undoubtedly this time he will hang himself."

In response, Ocean remarked, "In his prior existence, too, as Della said, I was somehow denied by him. This is the truth, and I have to face it."

When she was leaving, she noticed Collin in the terrace, who was looking at her with concern.

This time, she was considering on the drive home how she would explain the situation to her parents and why she had left Collin's house once more!

She was aware of one thing, though: her parents had never punished her for the choice she had made. They had always told her that she should learn from her mistakes and use them to enrich her life.

***

The house was completely different once Ocean went, as if she had stolen the house's spirit with her. This time, Mr. Criss was not going to let Della continue her dishonest behavior, so he instructed his attorney to bring an official complaint against her.

As Collin stopped going to work again and spent the entire day at home waiting for Della to call, he started to become irritable, violent, and depressed. She was supposed to reveal her address with Collin and move in together shortly, she had promised!

After spending a great night with Ocean, Collin was disappointed in how he behaved and wounded her. He knew he was upset that she had answered Della's phone, but it was not polite to let Ocean go. Oliva was preoccupied with organizing her wedding which made him feel quite lonely.

He just recognized what a fantastic person she was and how much he needed her emotionally after she drifted away.

After a few days passed without any updates from Della, Mr. Criss filed a complaint against her. As a result, the phone in Collin's bedroom as well as his own phone were being monitored by the police. This time, Mr. Criss was pursuing Della and he wasn't going to stop until he caught her.

Every day, Olivia would contact Ocean to check on how she was doing. However, because she wanted Ocean to make a decision this time, she never brought up the topic of Collin and his situation.

The doctors were worried about Collin and were attempting to find a solution for him by adjusting his medications and doing some tests; but, after Della showed up for real, he was also experiencing nightmares, leading Mr. Criss to decide to hire a caregiver, but this time for real.

The doctors wanted to start gently bringing up his background to help him grasp what is happening and what he is missing, but they preferred to keep the information about Della and Ocean out of the way because it was so upsetting for him to understand what was really going on.

Several groups of doctors and psychologists came to the house, but because he didn't want to see them and occasionally wouldn't leave his room, they had to leave without seeing him.

Ocean and her family were invited to Olivia's wedding party, which was scheduled to take place over the weekend. Olivia insisted that they attend because Darsh had threatened to postpone the ceremony if they didn't!

Collin was blushing at the breakfast table when Olivia told him that Ocean had also been invited. He was so excited that he couldn't finish his food.

"Is it okay if I call her and speak to her family on the phone? She must accept my sincere apologies," questioned Collin.

"I don't see any harm in calling to apologize, but if you'll pledge not to disrespect her again, I'll be very grateful. She's my friend, and Darsh really values her. She has done a lot for this family, and mother used to adore her, so please act like it!"

Collin hurried up the stairs like a young kid, looked at the time before calling Ocean's number—it was almost nine in the morning—and hoped she would answer.

"Good morning and hello."

"Mr. Roy, good morning. I'm Collin, how are you?"

"Oh Collin, how are you doing, my son? We're good, thanks. How about you?"

"I'm regretting what occurred the last time, Mr. Roy, and I want to explain. On occasion, I feel as though I'm losing control and I'll attack anyone who is in my sight."

"To be completely honest with you, if it were up to us, I would never permit her to enter your home, but she is a powerful, well-educated woman, and I want her to make her own judgments. I believe you should speak with her instead of me."

Collin was felling so shy to reply back and again he said, "It was a great pleasure to know Ocean and I am sorry again for not being a gentleman, please if it is fine with you and her mother, I want to speak with her!"

"No problem at all, I will connect the call to her room."

Collin was astounded by her parents' tolerance and protection. If only his father had been as supportive of his choice to wed Della, Collin's life would have been so much better.

Collin wanted to just stay on the phone with her and listen to her for hours since her voice was so soothing.

"Hello and good day, Mr. Collin."

"Hey, Ocean, how are you?"

Ocean was merely attempting to respond to his official inquiries, but she was secretly missing him.

"I don't know where to begin, but I am guilty of my behavior from the other day and I am very sorry. I hope I could somehow bring you back into my life, but not as my nurse, but as my friend, since we have shared so many wonderful moments together and it is hard to let them go."

"I do realize your medical problems and what happened to you in the past was unfair as well, but one thing I do not understand is," Ocean said after a little period of silence, "Each time your sweetheart, Ms. Della, calls, why do you quarrel or get furious with others? That day, I didn't even know you were home, so when the phone rang, I assumed it was you calling to ask for anything, and that is the full story."

"Ocean, you too have been in love and have experienced it, but for me it is different; I don't understand why I am pursuing her when I know she no longer wants me.

"Yesterday she said that my father had made her take some faked pictures of herself in a bridal gown and send them to me so I would stop wanting her."

After hastily checking to see if the door was shut, he returned and said, "I didn't get irritated at all when she was telling me these; I felt I had heard them before, and I was so okay with it, I didn't even care when she was telling me those.

"We shared a life, a history, and even planned the names of our future children, but I'm still not ready to let her go."

Ocean had to interrupt him because she couldn't stand to hear the remainder of his love tale. She knew he wanted to share, though.

"Please excuse me, I have to get to work right away."

"I was unaware that you began working at such a short period! What do you do and where are you employed?"

"I have a degree in digital marketing from Spain, took a sabbatical, and have recently opted to work with my dad because he needs my aid badly to grow his business."

"I'm not sure why I had the impression that you were in this line of work before you even told me about it.

"Would you attend the wedding of Olivia? She genuinely loves you!"

"Naturally, I am overjoyed for her and would want to attend her wedding."

"May I come and get you? Give me a chance, please!"

When Collin asked her that, she reacted with a blush, saying, "Sure, you can pick me up."

Chapter Nineteen
Truth in Your Eyes

Everyone spent the entire week working on wedding preparations in some capacity. Given that Olivia's mother had gone away, Olivia was asked not to have a lavish wedding. Instead, she planned to leave her home for a while and explore various countries.

From the day Collin confessed to Ocean over the phone, Ocean has been thrilled and overjoyed that at least Collin is now ready for a healthy relationship. For Ocean, this was the major goal of getting to know each other more intimately.

Ocean's parents were pleased to see that she was making an effort to look ahead. It was difficult for them to watch their one and only child suffer, but they felt that they had to allow her to go through everything because, even if it is painful, she will eventually learn!

Only a small number of their friends and family were invited to the ceremony, which was held at Darsh's residence.

This time, Ocean planned to dress in a way that would capture Collin's attention since she wanted to ensure that Della was out of the picture and show how much better-looking she could be with a little self-care.

"I think anything basic can do, you don't need to go to the extremes to capture his attention," Raya said, strongly against what her daughter was preparing.

"By looking at Della's images and styles, I realized how ostentatious she had been; by looking at her jewelry and her traditions in each shot, even her hair color and make up are unique. Apparently, Collin is so much in love of all these fanciness and if I follow her, he would end up loving me as well."

"I don't believe that's a smart move; you should just be yourself, so whoever desires you will want you for who you are," she said.

"No, Mom, you are mistaken, I was always me and he never wanted to have me; right now, he simply wants to be friends with me, which implies he is still wondering about Della, and I can't let that happen any longer. I have to struggle to get my boyfriend back, and I'm positive that this is the only way to draw other people of his sort."

Raya shook her head in protest, but she knew the argument had no chance of being heard. Raya was concerned that Ocean's plans would not turn out well.

Ocean purchased an extraordinary garment from a boutique two days prior; in her opinion, it was the most exquisite and expensive outfit in the entire town.

It was almost like a wedding gown, with a blue top that would turn white as it approached the bottom. It was also sleeveless and had plenty of laces before it reached the ground.

Her hairdresser was invited to meet her at home, and she was given instructions to purchase a small tiara to wear as head jewelry.

***

On the other hand, everyone was intending to wear something conventional and not overly fancy. Olivia and Darsh also had two sets of separate clothing in mind: one outfit for their ceremony in the temple and a second set in a bright white color for their reception.

Collin was attempting to select something eye-catching as well, but more than that, he was anxious about how to communicate his thoughts to Ocean and persuade her to stand by him without interfering with his connection with Della.

He sensed that Ocean and he had a deep connection, therefore he knew he wanted to be with her, but on the other hand, he didn't want to leave Della behind.

He was not at all concerned about falling in love with Ocean since, in his opinion, love can only happen once, and that was with Della. Instead, he wanted Ocean to be his friend, someone with whom he could share his feelings and chat about his issues and troubles with Della.

Ocean called Collin before he left the house to say that she would be attending the party by herself because she was still getting dressed.

Collin was a little let down because he had spent the entire week preparing and looking forward to it. He was still of the opinion that Ocean had not yet forgave him for his actions, or that perhaps her parents had convinced her otherwise.

Occan's parents were astonished to see how different she was acting. She refused to go with them to the temple for the ceremony when Mr. Aiden urged, she go, saying, "I don't think with these clothing I can fit in that place. Nevertheless, I will join you all for the reception."

The ceremony attendees were all on time, but Olivia was disappointed not to see Ocean there because she suspected that she might still be grieving. They swapped their wows after the two lovers were married. After an incredibly long time, Mr. Criss was the happiest person because he could finally see his daughter smiling.

After an hour, everyone was taken to the Darsh's home, where the real party was taking place. Collin was outside and there was still no sign from Ocean.

Then, a Mercedes drove by, and Ocean was the only person to emerge from it. Everyone else's attention was focused solely on her.

Collin ran in front to help her get down since he couldn't believe it was Ocean, saying, "Oh my, is that really you, Ms. Ocean? You appear incredible."

"Thanks, just a little self-care," Ocean responded with a smile.

She then moved in front, and Collin followed behind her. Collin was shocked to see her in that attitude since she reminded him too much of Della.

She went to the newly-weds and gave them her best wishes. The only person who appeared to be in favor of Ocean's outfit was Mr. Criss. "Collin will surely propose to you tonight itself, my beautiful Ocean, you truly nailed it tonight! I'm so impressed!"

Ocean was overjoyed to hear that, so she went and sat down at the table where her parents were already seated. Raya and Aiden were only grinning at her but were unable to comment on her appearance due to their disbelief that their daughter could make such foolish choices regarding her attire or makeup.

In order to have their first dance, the newly-weds were invited on the stage. Everyone burst into tears, especially Collin in particular, as a classic song that had been played during Olivia's parents' wedding came on.

The band welcomed everyone on stage for a dance after a short period of time during which the volunteers continued to serve drinks. Collin hesitated to ask Ocean to dance with him since he didn't want her to put any expectations on him.

Unaware of Collin and Ocean's past, another attractive man who was at the party went up and asked her to dance, and she readily agreed.

Collin was furious since he had not anticipated this sort of situation. Ocean made the decision to ignore Collin while dancing with another man because she wanted to make him jealous.

Collin was unable to handle it, so he first requested a bottle of wine, which he then began to drink despite being aware of how horrible it was making him feel.

"I'm dancing with a lady for the first time in this country, and she really knew how to dance," he said.

Ocean retorted to Rahul's statement, "I'm sure there are many girls who can dance better than me."

"I am Rahul, Darsh's best man, and we have been classmates since we were five years old. I apologize for not introducing myself. It was a pleasure for me to dance with such a lovely lady as you, and I hardly thought you were a citizen of this state."

Ocean was aware that Collin wanted to strike up a discussion with her, but she didn't want to blow her opportunity by spending time with Rahul. Instead, she wanted to let Collin know that while there are other males she could be with, she prefers to be with him.

She was looking intently at Collin when she noticed that he had begun drinking alcohol despite being banned to do so.

"I'm Ocean, and I'm sorry I have to leave right away. It was a great dance."

Collin noticed her leave and decided to follow her after she gave this excuse and went to the poolside.

She looked for a vacant location to sit in the packed area around the pool. The decision to wear such a fancy dress when practically rest of the guests were not dressed up at all caused Ocean to become agitated and uncomfortable in her gown. She then began to hate herself for her decision.

She turned to see Collin sitting next to her, looking at how angry and depressed he appeared to be at the same moment.

Ocean didn't want to start the conversation as they had both been sitting for a while when the servant had interrupted them by handing them some beverages.

Collin poured himself a glass of wine and one for Ocean. He then selected a cigar, lit it, and began to smoke.

"I don't think you should smoke or drink tonight; it is not advisable," Ocean warned, as she was concerned that what happened last time would happen again.

"What makes you care? I'm not even sure what to name you—Ocean or my second Della? How could you rationally justify turning to someone like her? You knew that I had no other need in the world but her love, and by dressing up to appear like her, you were trying to win my affection."

Ocean's face grew red, and she began to tremble and feel awkward in that outfit. Her entire strategy had failed, and she had been mistaken the entire time.

After finishing the drink, Collin stood up and stated, "The last few days, I've been working on my speeches in an effort to win your friendship and earn your trust, Nevertheless, tonight you showed me that you are just like everyone else and don't deserve my friendship at all. At least Della didn't try to be someone she wasn't, and I love her for that."

When Collin brought up Della's name once more, this time Ocean was vicious, and she was at her breaking point. She too rose to her feet, walked over to Collin, and said louder, "Everyone has been inviting me to fake who I am and what I'm doing in your lives all this time!

"They wanted me to act differently from who I am in order to make you happy and make them feel good; even your father, sister, and doctor forbade me, but tonight I realized it was a mistake. as you don't merit it."

Everyone around the pool turned to stare at Ocean when she said those words while some also began to video them on their phones.

Ocean continued, "I am Ocean Roy, born and raised in Spain, graduated in digital marketing, I worked in the office for you, and one day you just fired me, then the next day your parents forcibly made you come to my home to request me to marry you and you did that because you wanted to save your mother's life."

Collin's hands were trembling; he was about to have a heart attack from hearing what Ocean was saying.

Olivia and Darsh immediately hurried outdoors after hearing the news from someone! When Olivia approached to take Ocean away, Collin yelled at her, "Let her talk."

Ocean's parents were also present, and they requested that Ocean leave the party and accompany them. Ocean, however, resisted their request and stated, "I was dragged into this game, and performed a while but I didn't really fit in, so I have to complete it."

She continued, "On the eve of our engagement, your father hid the pictures of Della getting married in your closet," gazing directly at Collin.

"You discovered that the Della you were in love with was actually your blood sister when you spotted the voice recorder you had concealed in her home. She kept it a secret from you because she wanted to exploit you and ruin your family to get back at Criss.

"You just took a car and fled from everything that was going on and you got into an accident.

"And now you're in front of me saying that you still adore Della even if I'm not her! I'm really sorry, but you've started to fall for your own sister, Mr. Collin. Just wake up!"

Collin was out of control; he was smashing every glass on the tables and threw everything into the pool. When Mr. Criss and Darsh tried to stop him, he fled to his car and drove off.

Following her statements, Ocean collapsed unconscious to the ground.

Chapter Twenty
If Only I knew

Tragically, the wedding didn't have a suitable ending after that day, and nothing was the same.

Due to the event that occurred on the night of their wedding, Olivia and Darsh had to postpone their honeymoon. No one had heard from Collin in the past two days since he had been gone.

Mr. Criss kept calling Aiden to inquire about Ocean's health but received no response from either of them.

Time seemed to have stopped that night since nobody could move on with their lives until Collin and Ocean's relationship could be resolved.

The housemaids told Mr. Criss and Olivia of Collin's unexpected midnight arrival, and they both hurried to his room to speak with him.

Surprisingly, Collin didn't yell at them or demand that they leave his room as they had expected.

His eyes were merely showing fatigue, but his face was serene, as if he had just won. After all these years, he no longer resembled who he once was!

As she motioned for her dad to leave as well, Olivia remarked, "We simply come to check on you, it's better you rest and we can meet up at breakfast table!"

Collin answered to her, "Okay," while turning to face the outside of the window.

Even when Olivia and Mr. Criss left the room, they were unsure about what to do.

"Do you believe Collin is okay," Mr. Criss enquired? "Has he been able to recall the past? Should we continue to act as if nothing happened?"

"I'm the same as you, I have all these thoughts in my head too. I've even phoned his physician, and he said to only send him to the hospital if he is violent and his behaviors are uncontrollable," Olivia remarked as she was walking downstairs in response to her father.

"Dad, you will have to wait till the following day. At least we can be grateful that he is safe and sound at home!"

The following day, when Olivia and Mr. Criss arrived at the table, they noticed Collin was already seated and waiting for them.

"My son, good morning. how are you? Did you get enough rest last night?" While he was attempting to grab a chair and seat close to him, Mr. Criss questioned him.

Olivia went and sat down at the table a bit away from Collin after he asked the servant to bring tea for everyone while grinning at them.

"I haven't seen Darsh. Where is he?"

He received a response from Olivia, "He assumed he had to handle it himself until you or dad returned to work since he had been called to an urgent staff meeting early morning."

"Don't worry, I'll return to work very soon so he may take a well-deserved rest and take care of my sister," Collin replied after drinking a little of his tea.

No one spoke while eating breakfast; everyone was silent, the other two at the table had to wait for Collin to speak out so they could modify their behavior!

"Now that I'm fully awake and recall everything, I don't want to create arguments with anyone this time around. In fact, I regret my actions much more than before. Because of my insanity, my mother passed away, and I will live the rest of my life with a heavy burden of shame."

The fact that they could all act naturally without having to pretend relieved Olivia and Mr. Criss.

"I have lost the most important person in my life, who was my mother, and now I can feel the impact of her absence," Collin concluded.

"I wished I had been awakened sooner so I could have treated her with more kindness and niceness in her final few days."

When he started crying, the others also started to cry because it was such a delicate time for them all.

"What happened to Mum wasn't anyone's fault, it was her path, you can't even blame yourself for that, Mom was ill and sadly that caused her death," Olivia stated.

Collin stated, "Della was a decision I made for my life, and I don't want to hold Dad responsible.

"When she first entered my life, I could have seen so many faults in her and I kept quiet, thinking this is how love can begin and once we get married things get solved, but Della became very worse and I was urging to still be with her, I think she was even surprised why am I running after a girl like her!

"I have given everything a lot of thought over the past two days, but this time my eyes have been opened as well. I have come to terms with all the darkness I harbor and the harm I have done to my family. I find it incomprehensible that you would want me to pursue Della once more merely because I was still having memory issues.

"Although I claimed I didn't want to fight and that I wouldn't, I did want to know how far you two were willing to go before giving up. I was on the verge of being married to that crazy woman!

"I understand that everyone was doing their best to take care of me and follow the doctors' orders, but why did you all bring Ocean back into the picture this time? She was just an innocent girl that we attempted to manipulate for our own gain, not only myself but all of you as well!"

Since he was the one who first exposed Ocean to all of these games, Mr. Criss was the one who was experiencing the most sense of guilt.

"I know I've done wrong, but she was in love with you and none of us made her accept being with you. I could see how much she adored you and how eager she was to sacrifice everything to be by your side," Mr. Criss made a statement.

"Dad is right. Collin, you have no idea how much she endured for you, especially when all you talked to Ocean about was your connection with Della. At that time, this girl was sobbing within while outwardly pretending nothing had occurred and that everything was fine," Oliva stated.

Collin was speechless; Oliva's words simply struck a bell in his head and brought back the memory of the day he had taken Ocean out on a date; on the dance floor at the party, he had become disoriented once more and was addressing Ocean as Della.

He couldn't believe what he had done the night he returned from the party; he had destroyed Della's paintings in addition to all the staff in his room, and Ocean had been the one attempting to calm him down and clean up the mess.

He now realized that Ocean had always loved him and that he was the one she had claimed he had abandoned for another woman. He was shocked by the amount of suffering he must have caused her and by the way he had treated her throughout all of these instances!

Collin apologized for his behavior and left for his room since he was feeling exhausted, he wanted to be by himself, and he had a severe headache.

Collin wasn't sure how he could persuade Ocean that he no longer cared about Della and only desired to be with her.

This time, Collin was really serious, however he was hesitant to approach Mr. Aiden for permission to be with Ocean! How could he explain them that this time, he's really going to be with their daughter! Because this was what he wished, he was aware that he still had a long way to go he had to prepare for it.

A few days went by with no updates from Ocean. As the only people at Ocean's home were the housemaids, Collin and his father kept trying to phone and visit Ocean's home but never received a response.

After much insistence from Collin that they deserved a break and that he would take care of everything, Olivia and Darsh were finally able to take their honcymoon.

Everything that would have reminded Collin of Della, even pictures, was removed. The honey moon deluxe was no longer there because it had been converted into a guest bedroom.

He resumed his work routine, but this time he was accompanied by his father, who was managing everything with him. Mr. Criss was overjoyed to finally get his son back.

On his way home one day, Collin made the decision to stop by Ocean's house once more. Collin didn't tell his father and went straight there because he couldn't rest until he found Ocean.

He prayed every night for Ocean to come back into his life. He could now with certainty claim that he was in love with her, and he didn't want to waste any more time!

Collin attempted to scale the wall this time; he was aware that they were inside, but they refused to engage in conversation. The gardener and the rest of the house soon realized that Collin was there when their dogs in the garden began to bark!

Mr. Aiden swiftly entered the garden and requested them not to call the police when the gardener intended to. He was attempting to assist Collin with standing up on his own when he added, "You could be in trouble if we were not at home.

"I'm sorry I entered your home in such a manner, but please sir, I have to speak with Ocean." Collin stepped up and said while still holding his arm, "You folks didn't leave me any other choice and I had to do something."

After inviting him inside, Mr. Aiden asked the housekeeper to call Raya.

"I didn't know we had a guest, so how come you are here?" she exclaimed in wonder upon seeing Collin when she arrived downstairs.

"He has jumped over the wall and injured his arm. Will you aid him? It appears like his elbow is hurt," Mr. Aiden retorted.

Collin was reluctant to look into Raya's eyes as she approached, but he managed to say, "Mam, I am very sorry for breaking your house rule and don't worry, I will be alright, I had to talk with Ocean. Please allow me."

Raya told him to have a seat and requested that the servants get him some water. She was quiet, and Mr. Aiden was quiet as well. They were both staring at one another and were speechless.

Collin continued, "I'm back to normal, this is the real Collin. After that night, I started recalling everything, and I know who Ocean is and why I'm here today. I want to see her, and I wish to implore her forgiveness, please permit me to see her."

Raya answered him. "I am very happy that you are back to normal. I know your father is overjoyed right about now, but Ocean is not in the right frame of mind to accept you any longer. She is not feeling well, and we don't want her to get wounded more."

"I'm standing in front of you today ready for any penalty, but before that, would you kindly ask Ocean to speak with me? I'm sorry for everything, but I'm powerless to go back in time and fix all my mistakes."

"Ocean has recently been discharged from the hospital, and her health is not yet steady. Despite the fact that the doctor advised against it, we still wanted to bring her back to Spain as our kid is not in excellent health, we didn't want to express ourselves to anyone, so we avoided talking to them." As Raya wiped her tears away, she made a comment.

"We are taking responsibility for what happened to her; if we had been able to tell her no when she picked you from beginning, none of these things would have occurred! We gambled with her life!" said Mr. Aiden.

After hearing what they were saying, Collin became even more concerned. He had entirely forgotten about his arm and was attempting to persuade Ocean's parents to allow him to see Ocean.

"All these things are due to me and my family. I wish you had refused my father from the start, but there is no time to regret because I am here and I adore her.

"I'm here to bring my wife home with me; I want her so much. I've come to the realization that I was blind and lost in a previous relationship that served as a trap for me to exact revenge on my father. So, everything was twisted up, and after my accident, they didn't want to tell me what had occurred because they wanted to keep me alive. I lost my mother, and I'm still in mourning. Please, I implore you, let me see Ocean so I won't lose her too." While he was speaking those words, Collin was in tears.

Collin shivered as Raya requested him to follow her, and Raya observed that he was both excited and afraid. "You don't have to do this if you are not prepared. We don't want you to get involved with anything that is connected to Ocean. Please step back if still unsure."

"No, ma'am, I'm alright. I'm just overexcited and unable to control my feelings. In fact, this is the first time I'm seeing her since I truly developed feelings for her."

"I hope it's not already too late," Raya sighed and grinned glumly.

Next, she went to Ocean's room and opened the door. Raya went in first and told Collin to wait. The room was very dirty, the windows were closed, and it was quite dark.

As soon as Raya returned, she remarked, "She is lying down on her bed; you can enter, but don't startle her," and she went out.

Collin walked slowly and carefully, taking care not to make any noise. When he saw Ocean lying down, he briefly halted and wondered how he had been treating her so cruelly all this time. What a sweet girl.

He dragged a chair over and sat on it next to the bed because, above all else, he just wanted to enjoy seeing her.

He recalled the day when they went to the theater together. He was aware that Ocean's face was familiar to him and wished he knew more about her after treating her with such hatred. How could he forget those gorgeous eyes? Although knowing he was ailing, she returned for him and stayed to care for him.

She appeared to be extremely thin, and Collin moved in for a closer look while attempting to tuck Ocean's hair out of her face.

Ocean slowly opened her eyes and was startled to see him. At first, she was just staring at him, but then she sat on her bed and began to slink away, which led Collin to believe that she had been scared.

"Don't be frightened, I'm Collin, and I've come to see you, Ocean, my dear."

"How did you get into my room," Ocean asked as she put her hand in front of him to prevent him from approaching. "What are you looking for?"

"How can you not recognize me?" Collin repeated himself after becoming a little irritated. "Are you okay, Ocean?"

"I don't know who you are, and I am not Ocean, you are wrong!" Ocean hurriedly sprang out of her bed and began seeking a weapon to protect herself. When she found the umbrella, she held it out in front of him.

"I'm sorry I entered your room without your permission, but your parents are aware of my presence. Ocean, please accept my apology and have a seat so we can chat. I'm here to tell you how much I've thought about you through the past and how much I genuinely love you."

This time, Ocean threw the umbrella to the ground while claiming, "I told you, I am not Ocean, my name is Della, and I am in love with…"

She sat at the edge of her bed holding her head since she couldn't recall anyone's name. Collin swiftly walked over and sat next to her. He grabbed her hand, but she quickly drew it off.

Ocean started to head for the door, but Collin was there to stop her by running away. This time, he got too close to her and almost felt her breath. He then looked into her eyes once more and told her, "I'm sorry.

"I know I've done wrong and I definitely deserve it, but if I didn't want you, Ocean, I wouldn't be here. Please stop torturing me."

When Ocean struggled to open the door and attempted to force him into the corner once more, Collin began pleading with her by saying, "Ocean, stop. I'm sorry I wounded you so much, but just hear me before," he begged while sobbing.

She took a step back and turned to face him, saying, "My name is Della, my eyes are blue, and my hair is golden. I am in love with someone else, but I can't remember his name. Now that you know you're wrong, will you kindly leave me alone?"

"Your skin is tan, your hair and eyes are both black, and you look like the most beautiful person on earth."

"But I want my eyes to be blue why can't you realize, I am Della, even though I am cruel, but yet my fiancé wants me as he sees Ocean in my blue eyes! He will be coming for me because we are planning on marrying soon."

She began sobbing and screaming, "My love is coming for me. I wanted him so much, but he has not yet shown up. Where can he be?" As she sank down on the ground with her hands covering her face, she said, "I really hope he's not going to be with someone else."

Collin too sat on the ground, but this time he was closer to her. He attempted to hold her hand and whispered, "Your love is here and he has come for you. He is here to stay," while gazing into her eyes.

"This time, I want to be who he wants. I want to dress like he likes. I know he has preserved all the presents I have given him up to this point. I know everything. I want to be his forever, Della. And I know he already has my wedding gown in his closet. I can't wait to wear it."

Collin sobbed uncontrollably as he held her in his arms realizing what he had done…

THE END